One da
as Max
to show
becaus
lettering, ... technique comes before style and greatly affects the results
obtained.

Many of the co-workers in my studio have emerged
in schools in Zurich and Basel, young men who, by having
recourse to the rules and methodologies taught in those
schools, were able to find the right solutions to problems of
all descriptions. But it is the privilege of few, this natural
vocation that shapes the personality of those who possess
it and leads them to the acquisition of an original language
for the non-naturalistic transcription of aesthetic values.
Around every problem demanding an aesthetic choice
extends an area of personal feeling whose nature and intensity depend on the emotional and imaginative level of its
interpreter. Is it permissible for graphic designers to limit
their interest to their own work, to ephemeral fashions
and their excesses? Immersed as they are in the world of
visual communications, few of them have the strength
to escape from the confines of a convention that embraces
such fashions and accentuates their extravagances.

Bruno Monguzzi is one of these few. He belongs to the
group of keen defenders of functional and constructive
graphics so closely attached to the historical models of the
fathers of modern graphic art, whose validity has not been
impaired by the passage of time. From these models
he recovers that geometric spirit that so strongly marked
the essence and structures of the new typography.
His productions display the intent to place the object concerned in an ideal atmosphere and to reveal to us by
visual means its essential means. His work is consequently
not a realistic portrayal of the object that depends on an
immediate effect, but contains his own conceptual
interpretation. This means that this is not the aesthetic end
that decides his approach, which is suggested rather by
the nature of the object or message involved and accordingly
determines the visual factors: typeface, color, format,
paper quality.
This is an aesthetic position that will never be able to impose
itself and find effective expression without a cultural
background from which to draw its associations and ideas,
and thus to translate into images its interpreter's personal
vision of the world.

My close personal contact with Bruno has familiarized
me with the founts of information, the inquiring intelligence,
lively interest, and rich documentation of the works and
movements of culture by which his work is nourished and
justified. I admire the economy of his means, the very
natural way in which he expresses himself, the mental
reserve with which he keeps all mere show in check.[1]

Antonio Boggeri

1. Bruno Monguzzi," *Graphis* 209,
   vol. 36, 1980, pp. 256-61.

Bruno Monguzzi   **A Designer's Perspective**

This volume, the second title in the series
Issues in Cultural Theory,
is published in conjunction with

Bruno Monguzzi:
A Designer's Perspective

an exhibition organized by
the Fine Arts Gallery
University of Maryland
Baltimore County.

October 22, 1998
through January 16, 1999

Exhibition itinerary
in formation.

The music Jeu de Coincidence
was especially composed for the
exhibition by André Décosterd
and Nicolas Monguzzi.

Generous support
for the exhibition and publication
has come from
Pro Helvetia,
Arts Council of Switzerland
The Swiss Center Foundation
The Maryland State Arts Council

At UMBC
generous support
has been given from
The Office of the President
The Office of the Provost
The Office of the Dean of Arts & Sciences
The Office of Institutional Advancement.

Published by
the Fine Arts Gallery
University of Maryland
Baltimore County
Baltimore
Maryland 21250

Distributed by
Distributed Art Publishers
New York

ISBN 1-890761-01-X
ISSN 1521-1223

Contents

It has been a pleasure for me, as we prepared for this exhibition, to explore and experience the depth and breadth of the work of Bruno Monguzzi. When Franc Nunoo-Quarcoo approached me about this exhibition, I was interested, but had not had the opportunity to fully explore Monguzzi's work.

It is Bruno Monguzzi's ability to take the photographic image and synthesize it with typography as a complete and natural entity that makes his work outstanding in the contemporary practice of design. He engages the viewer to "read" the information as one image in the midst of many internal dialogues. These dialogues, dramatized in his careful constructions of the visual elements, form the spirit of the works.

It is this spirit that propels Bruno Monguzzi to be a great visionary.

David Yager
      Executive Director
      Fine Arts Gallery

I first became aware of Bruno Monguzzi when I worked in New York City for the office of the modernist American designer Rudolph de Harak. I usually spent my lunch hour poring over his many books in the open library area of the office. I still recall the neatly catalogued volumes on design, art, and architecture, and the dazzling pattern of the collective spines. There was one particular slender book, *RSt set*, that caught my eye. It is a modestly sized booklet on stainless steel cookware and flatware. What unfolded from the front cover continuing through the interior and onto the back cover was both typographic and photographic poetry in filmic sequence.

I first met Bruno Monguzzi in late October, 1988. He had come by the office to visit with Rudy de Harak. It was an evening, and almost everyone was gone. I was at my table working when in the near distance, I saw a spry, bearded man approaching. From me, he learned Rudy was away. We talked briefly about a set of translucent Schaedler rulers (which he admired) on my table. They are designed to be pliable, allowing one to measure around objects in addition to facilitating measurements in both metric and inches. A little while after meeting Bruno, I sent him a set of Schaedler rulers.

Almost ten years later, I telephoned him with a proposal to exhibit his work at the University of Maryland, Baltimore County, where I am currently Assistant Professor of Graphic Design. His generosity and enthusiasm have been encouraging to me and all involved in the project. My many demands of him were met with grace, humor, and expediency. Since the inception of the project, he has made two visits to the Fine Arts Gallery, to better understand the environment and the staff he was going to work with. Along the way, he designed the exhibition, announcement, and catalogue, and co-produced a video of his books specifically for this exhibition. His attention to detail and his informed and intuitive response to complex and complicated issues concerning this exhibition point to an individual with a gift and determination to providing both form and function to all he encounters.

This exercise has been for me an invaluable supplemental education, an experience I am sure to take into my classroom. I am very grateful.

Anna Monguzzi. She has come to symbolize to me an important figure in understanding Bruno Monguzzi. Her natural affinity for design and the fine arts is remarkable, especially because of her humility. Her ready smile and encouragement were invaluable to the realization of this project. I am equally grateful to her.

Large exhibitions of this kind must rely heavily on enlightened individuals and institutions for their generous support. At the Fine Arts Gallery, I am enormously grateful for the expertise and professionalism of the team of colleagues it takes to realize a project of this magnitude. First and foremost, I wish to extend my deepest gratitude to Professor David Yager, Executive Director of the Fine Arts Gallery, for his unconditional support over the past five years, and for the unique opportunity to realize this project through its long period of preparation. Symmes Gardner, Director of Programs, characteristically efficient and accessible, consistently provided enthusiastic support from the project's inception. He demonstrated unwavering patience and grace in his ability to cope with unforeseen issues and at the same time manage many other duties. Maurice Berger, Adjunct Curator of the Fine Arts Gallery and Editor of the Issues in Cultural Theory series, has been instrumental from the beginning with sound advice and constant support. Despite a demanding schedule, he always made time to teach and inspire me. Monika Graves, Projects Coordinator with enthusiasm, rigor, and pinpoint accuracy, attended to logistical concerns critical to this project. Toni Gardner, Managing Editor of the Issues in Cultural Theory series and editor of this particular volume, has my gratitude. She is a magician with the sensitive touch and expert guidance. Her commitment made it a pleasure in undertaking a project such as this.

I would especially like to thank the authors of the appreciations in this book whose significant contributions have greatly enriched the publication and my own understanding of Bruno Monguzzi's accomplishments: Dieter Bachmann, Pierluigi Cerri, Louis Danziger, Rudolph de Harak, Gene Federico, Marco Franciolli, April Greiman, and Ikko Tanaka.

At the University of Maryland, Baltimore County, I extend a special gratitude to President Freeman Hrabowski, Interim-Provost Arthur Johnson, and Dean Rick Welch, for their commitment to creating an environment for learning, research, teaching, and support of the Fine Arts Gallery. I would also like to thank Mark Behm, Vice President for Administrative Affairs, and Sheldon Caplis, Vice President for Institutional Advancement, for their continuous support of the Fine Arts Gallery.

I would like to acknowledge Pro Helvetia (Arts Council of Switzerland) for their generous support of the exhibition, the Maryland State Arts Council, Dr. Charles Zeigler, Director of the Swiss Center Foundation, for his support of the publication, and K.M. Kim of K Universal Air.

I also wish to thank my colleagues Peggy Re, Assistant Professor of Graphic Design, and Cynthia Wayne, Curator of Exhibitions at the Albin O. Kuhn Library and Gallery, for sharing the burden of being readers for the manuscript in the early stages of its preparation. On behalf of the Fine Arts Gallery and myself, I extend to Jennifer Phillips and Dina Wasmer our appreciation and gratitude.

Typographical design should
perform optically what the
speaker creates through voice
and gesture for his thoughts.[2]

El Lissitzky

If you keep shouting,
you are not making
communication any better.
You are only removing
talking and whispering
from the system.
I find our society a bit noisy.
I just would like
to contribute a little silence.[3]

Bruno Monguzzi

2. Sophie Lissitzky-Kuppers, *El Lissitzky*,
   Dresden: Veb Verlag der Kunst, 1967,
   pp. 360-64.
3. Ken Carls, *Contemporary Designers*,
   London: Macmillan Publishers, 1984,
   pp. 426-28.

Franc Nunoo-Quarcoo

Anna e Maria
The trees are still red.

Fine Arts Gallery
University of Maryland
Baltimore County
1998

As Event Co-Chairs of the Baltimore chapter of the American Institute of Graphic Arts (AIGA), they were instrumental in organizing with the Fine Arts Gallery the public programming of the exhibition. The participation of the AIGA underscores its commitment to visual communication.

I am grateful to the many individuals for their helpful contributions: Joanna Raczynska, for the exceptional video documentation of Bruno Monguzzi's books and for transcribing text; Tom Witt, for the beautifully fabricated tables, stands, and elements made specifically for the exhibition, Manuela Kahn-Rossi, Alberto Bianda, Nicolas Monguzzi, André Décosterd, Janet Rumbarger, Ugo Ugbor, Zahra Safavian, Mitchell Kim, Kenji Szczepanski, Satre Stuelke, Kevin Ley, Eileen Ragsdale, Jamie Summers, Scott Yoell, Brooke Singer, Yong-Ho Shin, Mark Raczynski, Lisa Akchin, Tom Moore, Julie Peoples, Mary Hess, Phyllis Addison, Ina Caplan, Charles McAree, Ellen Seeman and Carl Cox. On behalf of Bruno Monguzzi, I thank Aoi Huber-Kono, Susan Perkins, and Sergio Taiana.

I should like to thank Dr. Jo Ann Argersinger, former Provost of this institution and currently Chancellor of Southern Illinois University, for her understanding, interest, and support of design and its benefits to society. I am very appreciative. Finally, to Maria Phillips, I express my profound appreciation, love, and respect. I know you understand what I do better than I. I always enjoy learning from and listening to you.

Franc Nunoo-Quarcoo
　　　Assistant Professor
　　　Graphic Design
　　　Visual Arts Department
　　　University of Maryland
　　　Baltimore County

Appreciations

Before
the Great Flood.
Bruno Monguzzi
and
Switzerland

Dieter Bachmann
Arzo
August, 1998

Bruno Monguzzi sits under the loggia of his house and reads the newspaper. He sits at an old, well-scrubbed wooden table on a chair with a woven seat. If he were to look up, he would look into the inner courtyard of his farmhouse, he would see the courtyard, paved in a former century, the one-story coach house across from him, a multitude of healthy potted plants, and a large laurel tree. Behind him the three-story main building, renovated with cautious and sure taste, in which he has lived with Anna, Anna Boggeri from Milano, for more than twenty years, since his return from Lombardy to this southern-most part of southern Switzerland — from Milan, which can be seen from the edge of the woods on a clear day.

Bruno is wearing wide suspenders over a collarless shirt: he does not smoke and drinks quite moderately. Once in a while he has to go down into the valley with his small, red Peugeot, for a ten- or twenty- minute ride, to go shopping or go to work: go as a teacher to the shiny, new Accademia di Architettura in Mendrisio, or to Lugano, to the Museo Cantonale d'Arte, for which for many years he has created posters, prepared catalogues, and generally shaped its image. Considering that Bruno Monguzzi is a graphic artist and master of communication, and one of the few Swiss in this field who has achieved truly international stature and recognition, he leads a very average, normal life. When you look carefully at the man on his loggia, it becomes apparent that he cultivates this image a bit.

The red wine that now is on the table is sitting there in a bottle without a label: we can see again what a *bottle* is (the wine is table wine from Piemonte, from friends). Bruno wears a full beard. It makes him appear patriarchal. Once more, this cannot be a coincidence for a communication specialist. I have seen how he welcomed a woman by kissing her on the forehead while holding her head between his hands. By the way, it is impossible to imagine that Bruno Monguzzi would run after a bus, perhaps even with a briefcase in his hand, making a fool of himself in the city.

Here you live in the country and, yet, in a metropolitan area, an urban cosmopolitan area, which has everything that might detract from a pastoral life: a lot of industry, and lately a huge major airport (Milano-Malpensa); refugees; drugs; the metropolis of Milan and the major banking city of Lugano; a foundry for gold and a forest of petroleum depots and gas stations.

Bruno Monguzzi's village has ruins, empty houses, old people who have never been on an airplane; cows and deer (in an enclosure); households with no telephones, but with peace and quiet at night. It is a bit more than one mile, as the crow flies, to where the Stockholm-Palermo Expressway (N1, Basle-Chiasso) roars by, where the madness of annual migrations of vacationers surges on and on, where half of northern Europe rushes to the Mediterranean shore. Up here you sit in the grotto under paper lamps and under the stars, and you drink the local red wine from pottery cups, and maybe the men will sing old songs — while the inferno of the late industrial age rages beyond the next hill. Whoever lives here, lives with these contradictions…yet, it is against Swiss nature to live with contradictions. A Swiss is someone who has straightened things out.

You may ask yourself: What is Swiss about Bruno Monguzzi? And an immediate second question: What is Swiss about his work? Sure, he possesses a Swiss passport, and even Bertolt Brecht knew already: "The passport is the most important part of any human being." He has all Swiss citizenship rights and duties; and he is sure to have a Swiss bank account (which by now may, however, no longer represent the ultimate happiness to each and everyone). But: Albert Schweitzer, who in spite of his name was not Swiss, also had a beard and a somewhat remote work location. The most famous suspenders are not on Bruno Monguzzi's pants but on Bob Dylan's. And — to turn to something different — the best mountain cheese of the Tessin region is said to be available in New York — one of the riddles of export planning. The majority of Swiss do not want to join Europe, but a thoughtful minority of them does no longer want to be a "special case." To come straight to the point, wherever that which is Swiss appears to be interesting, it increasingly seems to be something that has been well-blended — and, hence, is not truly Swiss any longer. Again: Where is the "Svizzerità" of Bruno Monguzzi?

Is it represented in the *quality* of his work? A quality that would have to be described with words such as "care," "prudence," "clarity," "durability," "classicism"? These terms may indeed apply to the experts and masters of "Swiss graphic arts," ranging from Armin Hofmann via Müller-Brockmann and Karl Gerstner to Werner Jeker, Lars Müller, and specifically, to Bruno Monguzzi. Most of them, being theoreticians and teachers, have reflected on these concepts and have dwelled in them. But even if the Swiss would want it thus, quality is not an exclusively Swiss character- istic. The times when "Swiss graphic arts" were as unique as cheese exported from the Tessin region have passed. Perhaps there still might be something like a European sense of quality, which expresses itself in certain products (design) and campaigns (graphic arts) and in which high quality (that which is well thought out, appropriate) differentiates itself from the mass of mediocrity — yet, this is not Swiss privilege.

It is more to the point to see Bruno Monguzzi within the tradition from which he comes. If he is asked, he immediately mentions the name of El Lissitzky, in whom he admires the ability to present the story of his subject in the manner in which he implements the typographic construction, his unity of content and graphic communication. Unlike the popular, successful graphics products (… as much noise as possible at the speed of Quark Xpress…),

Monguzzi's work does not initially focus on the aesthetics but rather on the substance at issue, and then he tries to elicit from it the appropriate aesthetics required for it. Bruno Monguzzi has said that his work, the work of communication, is to "present contents with as little distraction as possible to as many people as possible." Those who know him know that the emphasis in the sentence rests on the word "contents." These ideas have also been described by the term "Bauhaus." Bruno has said that later this tradition had, however, become petrified at the Hochschule für Gestaltung (Academy for Design) in Ulm. It may be surmised that this is precisely the reason Bruno Monguzzi prefers a connection to the Russians, to constructivism: aesthetics as the expression of a societal obligation.

The Swiss in such an approach would be typified by the aspect of preservation. In light of the great flood of vainglorious exercises in style (exemplified by the prevailing aesthetics of magazines, i.e., as much computer noise as possible with as little content as possible) it would be an attempt not to exhibit *style* but *attitude*! This immediately takes us to the question of his working method. In fact, we see no influence of electronic data processing in Bruno Monguzzi's work. He is the last inhabitant of the world of pencils. If he shows his method of working at all, perhaps during an exhibition, one can see how he continues to handle his pens, scissors, papers, and materials in general. The immaterial aspect of the computer apparently does not suit him, which in turn has the consequence that his work, for example his posters, always exudes a very tactile quality. It becomes literally graspable in catalogues, when Bruno Monguzzi has the pages arranged and folded in such a way that a type of Leporello is created of printed and unprinted pages, so that the carrier medium of information, the *paper* itself, becomes apparent. Or when he makes the *material* used for packaging, for example the carton for kitchen utensils of the Rstset company, clearly become apparent as such. I think that this characteristic could be called Swiss in the sense that at the end of the industrial age and as part of industrial production Monguzzi is able to draw our attention to the *skilled artisanship*.

Is it possible that in this way the Swiss ability to persevere, the country's extreme conservatism of values, would appear not as a handicap, a hindrance, for once, but instead as stabilizing, even productive? That one more time "good" graphic communication and presence (a moral term used here intentionally) wins before everything ultimately takes the path of least resistance: of complete loss of responsibility and remembering? Or that in this case that which is conservative still has the appearance of the avant garde? And is not merely a continuation of constructivism, but is a constructive here and now?

Irrespective of how these questions may be answered, Bruno

Monguzzi not only has a flexible mind, he also has been lucky.
The quality of his assignments is not commonplace — Museo
Cantonale d'Arte! And what a lucky man he is who understands
to respond in turn with quality. And Bruno Monguzzi is lucky in
his choice of where to live. Yes, precisely here, under the loggia of
his venerable house and in a village, which in its local museum has
preserved the fossils from before the great flood, i.e. lizards,
dinosaurs, and reptiles from the Jura Sea… Here, in the bustling
region of northern Lombardy, within the culturally sleepy Svizzera
Italiana, there is a niche where one can live with one's contradictions. More than that: Where one can be a radical by being
a conservator.

An outrageous
act

Pierluigi Cerri
Milan
April, 1992

Is the approach I take when interpreting a graphic image the same
approach the artist followed when he designed it?
How is it possible to gain a clear insight into how the system
of interconnections and interrelationships among the parts, the
geometric arrangements, and the rules governing their creation
have come together to produce that particular text or image?
And what are the degrees of interpretive freedom?
Bruno Monguzzi is a designer firmly rooted in modernism.
He possesses a very rare quality that allows him to impart
a spontaneous inductive and deductive clarity on every project,
no matter how radical or marginal.
In each of his projects, the core always shines through, the very
heart of the intuition that created the chain of relationships
that "are" that object.
The realization of that object, via the interconnections among
the rules of production, the aesthetic processes, and the manifes-
tation of interpretive conventions, is in essence the first rule
of the historical avant-gardes, which Bruno Monguzzi views with
unconcealed emotion, as well as a certain scientific detachment.
One could compose expansive arabesques in praise of his
graphic talents.
When he was very young he found his vocation alongside Aldo
Calabresi, as somewhat of a child prodigy in the Boggeri studio.
He then traveled widely throughout the world, ending up as
a learned and much-loved professor in the hermitage-like setting
of Meride (Switzerland).
But what interests us here is how he manages to transform
a graphic composition into an intensely poetic object. How can
a railroad "timetable," beyond its function of explicitly portraying
the routes through the region with diagrammatic clarity, be
more beautiful than every other railroad timetable?
Can a map represent a territory without reproducing it, but rather
by subjugating it to a will of abstraction that yields back
conceptually the flow of matter and information via a new formal
logic? What formal logic, what aesthetic value, what beauty
does it entail?
A page is communicated in all its clarity when measured by
an invisible grid that partitions the surface, creating a foundation
that allows it to be read according to a well-defined scheme,
any breach of which stands out as a deviation.
Paradoxically, the history of modern graphics can be read as
a succession of necessary deviations. The deviations in the work
of Bruno Monguzzi are not obvious, but I know of no other work
that is more transgressive, while at the same time so resolutely
rational.
Monguzzi has contrived an outrageous act within the conformity
of the graphic work. He has raised for discussion the autonomy
of writing with respect to graphics.

He doesn't merely arrange columns of characters in the right positions.

He doesn't enclose his texts in cages, but rather designs them, interprets them, makes them part of the visual process, manipulates them in "rigorous dependence." He composes them on the page after having thought through how the page serves as a foundation that interacts through its material composition, its color, its "tactility."

The compositional degrees of freedom of Bruno Monguzzi lie in this conceptual coalescence, in his technical knowledge, in his inductive capacity, in his ability to synthesize, and above all, in that frontier on which he realizes the most mysterious part of the project — that which creates poetry out of even the most insignificant aspect of the message.[1]

22   1. *Bruno Monguzzi*
Maison du livre de l'image et du son,
Villeurbanne, Lyon, 1992, p. 2.

The more
you look, the more
you see

Louis Danziger
Los Angeles
June, 1998

Bruno Monguzzi's work is immediately successful and is appreciated by all audiences, but it is deceptively simple. As in the appreciation of great music, the layman's perceptions are different than those of the skilled musician. The layman responds and is moved by the music, but is unaware of what is going on. The magic, the subtleties, the understanding, and the historical contextual knowledge are unavailable to the untrained ear. Monguzzi's greatness is most appreciated by the design practitioner; to the connoisseur the work is profound.

First, the piece is always visually arresting. It attracts and captures the eye. It immediately signals its unique presence. It has a sense of "rightness" about it. It seems to be a perfect fit for the subject it deals with. The very first glance tells you that this piece holds the promise of meaning, that this beautifully structured work is a product of care, of intelligence and unfathomable talent. What I find particularly interesting in Bruno's work are the constant paradoxes and contradictions. It appears to be (as is typical of much Swiss work) meticulously orderly, everything in its place, everything at just the right size, every hair in place, nothing left to chance. Yet it is so expressive, so poetic, so rooted in the ineffabilities of the subject. Like mysterious African sculpture there is some moving presence in there. The more you look, the more you see.

His work is simultaneously orderly yet spontaneous, sensuous yet cerebral. I find it fascinating. I often try to figure out what is going on, how does he do it? I think it has something to do with his visceral response to the subject, be it furniture, work of art, or a photograph of a weeping woman. He is all empathy, and then he proceeds to use his intelligence and craft to manifest these feelings for the viewer, to give them a visual presence.

It is not just the meaning of content which he wishes to manifest, that is always a given — it must communicate, but for him that is insufficient if it does not also touch you with the expressive feelings, his sensitivities to the subject. It is so human, a mix of head and heart. It is why I like his work and of course that's why I like him so much.

The International Typographic Style (also known as Swiss Design) came to life as a powerful and influential movement in Germany and Switzerland shortly after the Second World War. The designers involved in this design philosophy worked within a common syntax. They sought a pure graphic communication through an objective and impersonal presentation of information, devoid of subjective feelings and propagandistic techniques of persuasion. Their almost exclusive use of the typefaces Akzidenz Grotesk and Helvetica consisted of strong asymmetric compositions and powerful black-and-white presentations of images. Because their graphic vocabulary was so similar, it could at times be difficult to identify the author of a particular piece of work, even for those quite familiar with the work of the best designers.

Leaders in the Swiss movement, such as Max Bill, Armin Hofmann, Josef Müller-Brockmann, Carlo Vivarelli, Siegfried Odermatt, Rosmarie Tissi, Richard Lohse, Hans Neuburg, Carl B. Graf, and Karl Gerstner, to a name a few of the best, established a pure design criteria that became the standard by which almost all graphic design was measured for the next twenty years.

Their influence was felt as far away as the United States and Japan. This dynamic design philosophy didn't develop from just thin air. It found its beginnings in the manifestos of de Stijl, the Bauhaus, and Jan Tschichold, who perhaps did more to liberate type from its entrenched conservatism than any typographer/designer of that time. Tschichold's writings on design, *Die Neue Typographie* (Berlin 1928) and *Typographische Gestaltung* (Basel 1935), had tremendous impact on the Swiss and German design and typographic communities. The 1935 book was later published in English as *Asymmetric Typography*. Tschichold wrote:

"Sans serif is more expressive than any other face because of its wide range of weights (light, medium, bold, extra bold, italics)."

"… so, in the beginning of the twentieth century, a remedy was seen in using, in a particular job, different sizes of one and the same type face only. This was called Einheit der Schrift (unity of type)."

Strangely, in 1946, Tschichold, having emigrated to England, reversed his extreme philosophic position on the use of asymmetric typography and gave his full support to a revitalization of the use of classical typefaces and layout.

Bruno Monguzzi's work, while clearly showing the influences of the International Typographic Style, has a spirit that transcends the objectivity and impersonal thrust common to that movement. It never quite fits the same mold. That is, Bruno seems to respond to the rules, but somehow his emotional and human side enters into the design process, with the result that his work expresses a warmth uncommon to so much of the work by other designers of the Swiss School and becomes highly personal.

Bruno Monguzzi:
a not-so-Swiss designer

Rudolph de Harak
Elsworth, Maine
May, 1998

1

2

3

4

Yet the interesting point here is that his work appears devoid of a specific style. It is difficult to identify a Monguzzi design, because his design solutions have no preconceived matrix.

Theoretically, each piece could have been done by a different designer. Perhaps the best way to identify a Monguzzi piece is by the brilliance of the conceptual idea and the consummate skill and technique applied to its realization. Time after time, he brings this extraordinary skill to his visual problem solving. Few designers can achieve this level so consistently.

It is in this context that the manifestations of his design philosophies are in closer accord and can best be compared to the early (1930s) work of the Swiss designer Ernst Keller, whose designs strongly expressed content rather than emphasizing a consistent style or system. Additionally, the work of Herbert Matter, also a Swiss designer and photographer who later migrated to the United States, was of equal importance to Monguzzi, but from a different perspective. Matter's graphic design, augmented by his photography, was in many ways ahead of its time.

His strong photography and dynamic photomontages had the capacity to turn one's orientation of space topsy-turvy. Matter could almost literally put the viewer on a roller coaster, simultaneously experiencing space and perspective from conflicting points of view. While influenced by artists such as Herbert Matter, Ernst Keller, El Lissitzky, and others, the manifestations of Bruno Monguzzi's graphic design are entirely different. Creatively, he is without question his own person.

Could it simply be that his having been born in Ticino, the Italian section of the Alps, accounts for that strong, emotional part of him and that much of his need to communicate on a human scale, and being Swiss helps to explain that great care and exactness in his work?

Bruno came into this world at an extraordinary period of our history, just at the time that all of Europe was in war and chaos. Later, in the mid 1950s, just prior to entering into his teens, he began developing meaningful insights into the world about him. He had ideas about becoming an architect, but at the age of sixteen began instead his studies of graphic design at the École des Arts Décoratifs in Geneva. Here he became acutely aware of the potentialities of design and those practicing it.

He was greatly impressed with and influenced by the designers mentioned earlier and by the pioneers of modern movements of the previous generation. However, I would speculate that Bruno's most deeply felt and lasting reactions were to El Lissitzky. The Russian constructivist's 1924 *Self Portrait*, his 1929 *Russische Ausstellung* poster, the photographic technique employed by his Pelikan advertisement of 1924, and his *Prouns,* among others, must have made an indelible imprint upon his impressionable soul. The international spirit of Monguzzi's work in his formative years

1. Carlo Vivarelli
   For the Elderly, poster, 1959.
2. Jan Tschichold
   Mailing label, 1929.
3. El Lissitzky
   Self-portrait, 1924.
4. El Lissitzky
   Pelikan advertisement, 1924.

owes much to his studies in London, his work in Milan for Antonio Boggeri, and while there, exposure to some of Italy's most influential graphic designers, including Franco Grignani, Max Huber, Giovanni Pintori, and Albe Steiner. This was followed by important work at Montreal's World's Fair, Expo '67, and in the United States. The common thread tying Bruno Monguzzi's work together is evident in the deep thought and care that goes into every aspect of a design. His work shows a predominant concern for the development of a unique theme or conceptual approach that is sensitively integrated into the design. Every element of the design is given careful consideration, including scale, figure/ ground, type choice and size, cropping of photographs, and color relationships. Perhaps most important is his uncanny ability to anticipate how much to leave out so that the viewer can subliminally fill in the blanks and psychologically feel a sense of participation with the designer.

In a discussion of his work philosophies, Bruno stated that his interest in the Swiss approach to design ultimately suffered because "… it was so rigid in syntax that it was, in some cases, no longer functional." Nevertheless, within this rejection there is, in my opinion, always an underlying structure that could only be the consequence of his early exposure to Swiss design. In the 1970s, with the establishment of the Post-Modern style, there was a distinct movement away from the International Style. Curiously, this was precipitated by the Swiss. As a consequence, some very different and interesting work developed. Many of the major designers didn't become involved in the Post-Modern style in any conspicuous way but continued to work in a manner that was most comfortable to them. Certainly, no apparent change is evident in the work of Monguzzi. Coming in contact with his work only reinforces the understanding that style per se is not the primary issue.

Bruno Monguzzi has made a very important contribution to the field of visual communication. His work is admired and influential not only in his own country and in Europe, but certainly in the United States and Japan. With the frequent superficiality and hit-or-miss quality of so much graphic design we experience today, we need more graphic designers like him, who bring an honesty, integrity, and unique quality of timeless creativity to their work.

5

5. Franco Grignani
   Advertisement for Alfieri & Lacroix, 1960.

Bruno Monguzzi

Gene Federico
Pound Ridge, New York
1998

Being a teacher, Bruno Monguzzi is rarely at a loss for language. So it is hardly surprising that his all-consuming passion is to be found in the pursuit of his lifetime search for the universal language vis-à-vis Graphic Design. And, for Bruno Monguzzi, given our brief candle, the intensity of this passion is underscored by the positive and innovative answers to his search.

I first met Bruno Monguzzi on a sleek Pentagram-designed British Railway coach out of Paddington Station headed for Bath, the designated venue for the 1978 AGI Congress. He came as a guest of Roberto Sambonet, a member of the Italian contingent of the AGI. At the members' exhibition, Sambonet showed a work containing a series of drawings he had made of the faces of inmates in a Brazilian mental institution in 1952. The drawings were printed as part of a two-section presentation entitled *Della Pazzia* — part 1) the many faces of insanity as drawn by Sambonet, and part 2) insanity as found in literature and music, and these examples were designed by Monguzzi. This piece was put together in a magnificent 13- by 19-inch boxed presentation of such dazzling elegance because elegance was such an integral part of the whole communication (contrasting the elegance of Art and the stylization of insanity vs. the truly desperate nature of real insanity). The use of the word "elegant" is used here in the same manner in which a well-turned mathe-matical equation or a superbly executed chess maneuver is termed "elegant." I was astounded by the virtuosity of the piece, virtuosity tightly knitted into appropriateness. No loose ends. Whatever means were employed had to bear significantly on the whole. As true an expression of Gestalt as I had ever seen.

This meeting in Bath led to a friendship I hold very closely. It led to an understanding of Monguzzi's method in his work and the method in his life. But to return to *Della Pazzia* — the initial impact this work had on me has never diminished on being confronted with later works of Monguzzi. The opening piece from Euripides, fifth century B.C., in Greek. Letterpressed on high-gloss stock. It contrasts with the second piece dated 1532 by Ariosto, in Italian. Offset initials of each line in Roman. The remainder of the line set in Italics.

All placed high on the page. Then Shakespeare, 1606. Coarse laid stock, Stag watermarked. A play. Act III, King Lear. Mad Chinese-red type rules structuring this Scene VI. A typeface with the look of old in a modern master's hand. And later, a piece by Voltaire, 1764. Truly exquisite typography where even the widows have been designed. Essence of French. Then Donizetti, 1835. A sheet of the music from the mad scene of Lucia di Lammermoor. And so on. A total of twenty examples of visual delights, so perceptive of the time and place in which the pieces were originally written. This whole work must be held in hand. Word description falls far too short.

101

The exhibition of the times and works of Majakovskij, Mejerchol'd, and Stanislavskij mounted in the Castello Sforzesco, Milan, 1975,

was accompanied by a superb catalogue designed by Monguzzi. Using a strong grid on an almost square format he created a 128-page catalogue which had the essential feel of Russia in the early years of the century. But the presentation in the hands of Monguzzi was unquestionably of our time. He designed a system of heavy type rules tightly containing type and pictures. The rules used were of three weights. The heavier rules running down two-thirds of the upper outer edge of the spreads — the heaviest rule identifying the sections devoted to Majakovskij, Mejerchol'd, and Stanislavskij — with the page numbers at the base of these peripheral rules, left and right. These same rules created an additional accent on the edge of the book when closed. The book was bound in red cloth and the black edging and white paper projected a clear and powerful image of the nature of the contents. This is orchestration of the highest order. Of type, graphics, space. This is the Monguzzi system of working — always juggling to crystallize the very singularity of form and content.

And never was the "What, Where, When" duty of the poster so expertly performed as in the magnificent ongoing series conceived by Monguzzi for a public institution, the Museo Cantonale d'Arte, Lugano. A statement by Cassandre comes to mind — "Le spectacle dans la rue." The Monguzzi posters are street communication at its most impressive. Informational, elegant, bombastic, magnetic. Always a great light on any city thoroughfare.

Monguzzi takes hold of your eye with an initial onslaught of beauty, then sense, then he hands you the gift of intellectual communication. The consistency of his work, however, given the nature of his working method, avoids the pitfalls of personal style. Each work stands on its own intelligence, clarity, and grace. The only constant in his body of work appears to be his method. This method, which he once explained to me in simple terms, is to trisect the problem thusly: probe the semantic aspects, clarify the syntactic needs, and finally, develop the pragmatic application.

On viewing a Monguzzi work, I come prepared with what I know. I know to come prepared to learn. The more I know, the more I learn. And the least that can be said of Monguzzi is complete comprehension of the role of the designer as a culture medium which transcends time boundaries.

Bruno Monguzzi
and the
Museo Cantonale d'Arte
of Lugano

Marco Franciolli
Lugano
September, 1998

In 1997 the Museo Cantonale d'Arte dedicated its exhibition program to the celebration of its first ten years of cultural activity. On this occasion, a tribute was paid to Bruno Monguzzi with an exhibit of the posters, catalogues, and projects he has designed for the museum. The show revealed the cohesiveness of the image of the Museo Cantonale d'Arte that he created, an image characterized by essentiality and intelligence. We are delighted that now, thanks to the enthusiasm of Franc Nunoo-Quarcoo and the support of the University of Maryland, Baltimore County, a travelling exhibition will allow the extraordinary work of Monguzzi to be seen in the United States.

The creation of a new museum requires thoughtful choices in all facets of appearance and in every undertaking, as these choices contribute to defining the museum's identity.

Visual communication is fundamental to convey this identity as it must reflect, in its complexity, the cultural policy adopted by the museum. The decision to entrust such a task to Bruno Monguzzi was made with an awareness of the particular needs of a museum in the very first years of its existence. The choice was also motivated by the corresponding desire to benefit from collaborating with a strong personality — a designer with extensive experience who was, above all, capable of projecting a meaningful, immediately recognizable image.

Over ten years, Monguzzi has been able to interpret, synthesize, and communicate visually the contents and meaning of the museum's various initiatives. Excluding certain "extraneous" publications, catalogues for international distribution requiring significant editorial and financial resources, the image of the Museo Cantonale d'Arte was created entirely by Bruno Monguzzi: posters, catalogues, invitations, signage.

This was made possible through an intense and stimulating collaboration between the designer and the museum's management. Over the years, Monguzzi has made an enormous commitment to the Museo Cantonale d'Arte. Only those who have had occasion to observe his work methods close up can appreciate the magnitude of his commitment. His method involves developing the conceptual aspects as well as more practical aspects, from a perspective that flattens traditional hierarchies, while his capacity to worry simultaneously about the seemingly trivial details allows him to have total control, yielding a final result of unmistakable quality.

The museum's posters and publications have been awarded numerous Swiss and international prizes. Such recognition is a valuable vehicle for publicizing the activities of a "young" museum and is a positive indication of a partnership between a museum and its designer that has turned out to be profitable and rewarding over the years.

The first year I was admitted into the "old boys club of design,"
the Alliance Graphique Internationale (AGI), I was asked
to present my work at the upcoming congress in Switzerland.
I was nervous alright. My qualifications and seriousness of intent
had been questioned for a number of years already, prior to my
being elected a member. (… "She is an artist, not a graphic
designer, … Give her five years and if she is still in business" … ,
"She is too young," etc.) All of my kings (and a few queens) would
be there in the audience. Definitely my detractors would show
up for this one! Phew!

So, here I am, in Switzerland, with the best technology they had
to offer. My presentation is a home-made soundtrack, two
slide projectors, and a dissolve unit. Showtime! I present to the
audience of over one hundred members and their guests.
Now that the presentation is over, pulled off flawlessly by
the Swiss technicians. I am sighing a huge sigh. I am proud to be
a member. Then the war starts… "Your work is so slick… too
Hollywood… your earlier work of the late '70s was better… the
new work is cold… " I am in shreds. Then *suddenly*, from the
audience, a different energy and voice. A bearded man comes
running up to the podium, where I am dissolving into my emotional
puddle of despair… "Brava, bellissimo, grazie Aprile!" It is Bruno.
The man who saved my life in that moment in Switzerland.
Our first meeting. Since then I have looked for him annually,
at these gatherings, to renew my faith in what's best about being
a human and in design.

Now! Bruno's design work is — sensual yet spare, heady yet
warm, serious with levity. Juicy. Tiramisù served with Roederer
Cristal.

He is an artist. He is so young. He has been doing it for at least five
years. Bravo, bellissimo, grazie Bruno! (Do you have any
brothers?)

"Brava,
bellissimo,
grazie
Aprile!"

April Greiman
Los Angeles
June, 1998

Monguzzi:
poems
of artistic form

Ikko Tanaka
Tokyo
July, 1998

The Presence of Absence: The Photograms in 20th Century Art,
a prize winner at the 1991 Toyama Poster Triennal, was my first
encounter with a poster by Bruno Monguzzi. The first impression
I had was of the cleanness of the image. There was a dignity that
made it unapproachable.

Monguzzi's works are deeply rooted in the Swiss tradition of
modern typography, but they don't look old or dated in the least.
Each piece is a masterwork of expression, imparting a sense
of freshness and emotion combined with intelligence. Bold and
powerful structures blend with incredible intricacy to create
beautiful music.

When examined closely, Monguzzi's design style is free of waste.
He identifies the core elements of the message and embodies
it in a splendid and powerful form. One can see that no effort was
spared in communicating the theme itself without allowing the
personality of the artist to intrude on the work itself. For example,
one can appreciate the careful attention given by the artist to
the selection of the typefaces, which is obvious even to a designer
like myself from a country that uses kanji.

A world away from the hustle and bustle of Tokyo, Monguzzi's
works carry with them the clean air of the lake of Lugano. Yet they
also express just a hint of lunacy. As in the posters of Museo
Cantonale d'Arte, he weaves together a collage from pieces of
ordinary photos, pictures, and letters into an artwork as if he were
a magician. He is an amazing artist whose designs emanate
poetry.

Dieter Bachmann, born in 1940 at the other extreme end of Switzerland, in Basel, is a freelance writer and journalist. He was editor in chief of the European cultural magazine *du* from 1988 until 1998.
> Translated from the German by Brigitta M. Richman

Pierluigi Cerri graduated in architecture from the Milan Polytechnic, where he also taught. He was art director of the Bienniale of Venice in 1976 and Electa Editrice publishing house. He is editor of *Casabella* and *Rassegna* magazines, among other publications. He has designed numerous books, including the Italian edition of *Vers une architecture* and the interactive series *Encyclomedia*, directed by Umberto Eco. He has designed exhibitions for museums and galleries throughout Europe and is responsible for the interior design of a series of ocean liners and the architectural design of the Prada buildings in Italy and the U.S. Cerris's designs include furniture, lighting, television sets, and the publicity for the Italia 90 World Soccer Championship. In 1998 he established Cerri & Associati in Milan.
> Translated from the Italian by Gerard H. Heller

Louis Danziger has been an art director, designer, and consultant working out of Los Angeles since 1949. Long-term clients include the Atlantic Richfield Company, the National Endowment for the Arts' Federal Design Improvement Program, the NEA's Design Arts Awards Panel, the Dreyfus Agency, and the Los Angeles County Museum of Art. In addition to conducting numerous visiting lectures and workshops, Danziger has taught extensively at the Chouinard Art Institute, the California Institute of the Arts, Harvard University, and the Osaka Communication Arts and Tokyo Communication Arts schools in Japan. Danziger's work has been exhibited throughout the world and is in the collections of the Museum of Modern Art (New York), the Library of Congress, and the Los Angeles County Museum of Art.

Rudolph de Harak has been a graphic designer, photographer, and painter based in New York since 1946 and a teacher and lecturer on design since 1952. de Harak has received many awards for his work, which has been featured in publications, museums, and exhibitions throughout the world. He received the American Institute of Graphic Arts Gold Medal and has been inducted into the Art Directors Hall of Fame. de Harak is the Frank Stanton Professor of Design Emeritus at the Cooper Union School for the Advancement of Science and Art, where he began teaching in 1952. The Frank Stanton chair is the first permanently endowed design chair in the U.S. He has also taught and lectured at many institutions throughout the U.S. and in Canada and England. His clients have included the Metropolitan Museum of Art, IBM, and Columbia Records. de Harak lives in Maine where he pursues his various interests in the arts.

Gene Federico graduated from the Pratt Institute in 1939. Since 1945 he has served as art director for, among others, Grey Advertising, Doyle Dane Bernbach Advertising, and Benton & Bowles Advertising. In 1967 he co-founded Lord, Geller, Federico, Einstein, Inc. Advertising, where he remained until 1989. He has been a board or committee member of the New York Art Directors Club, the American Institute of Graphic Arts (AIGA), the Alliance Graphique Internationale (AGI), and the Cooper Union's Herbert Lubalin Study Center of Design and Typography. His work is in the poster and card collection of the Museum of Modern Art (New York) and in the Graphic Design collection of the Library of Congress. Federico is currently an independent consultant in advertising and graphic design in Pound Ridge, New York.

Marco Franciolli has been curator of the Museo Cantonale d'Arte since 1989. He studied painting and art history at the Accademia di Belle Arti in Florence, graduating in 1981. In Bern he produced classical music programming for radio, and he studied at the London International Film School. He regularly organizes exhibitions specializing in contemporary art and photography and lectures on art history and museum administration both in Switzerland and abroad.
> Translated from the Italian by Gerard H. Heller

April Greiman graduated from the Kansas City Art Institute in 1970 and studied at the Allgemeine Kunst Gewerbeschule in Basel, Switzerland. Her work includes projects with architects Barton Myers, Kaplan McLaughlin Diaz, Morphosis, and Roto Architects, directing the Visual Communications Program at the California Institute of the Arts, and teaching at the Southern California Institute of Architecture, where she is currently an instructor. She has served on the USA Expert Jury for numerous competitions, including China's First International Graphic Design Competition in Beijing in 1996. Greiman's work has been exhibited in museums in the U.S., Japan, Europe, Israel, and the Soviet Union.

Ikko Tanaka graduated from the Kyoto City College of Fine Arts in 1950. After design work for the Kanebo Co., Ltd., the Osaka Sankei Shimbun Co., Ltd, and the Nippon Design Center, he founded the Ikko Tanaka Design Studio in 1963. He has received numerous awards in Japan and throughout the world, including Poland, France, Italy, Mexico, and the U.S. He is chairman of the Tokyo Art Directors Club. Publications include *The Work of Ikko Tanaka*, *The Design World of Ikko Tanaka*, *Surroundings of Design*, and *Front, Back, Right and Left of Design*. Tanaka's work is represented in the collections of the Stedelijk Museum in the Netherlands, the Museum of Modern Art (New York), and the Kyoto Institute of Technology, among others.
> Translated from the Japanese by Harumi Rudolph

A Poet of Form and Function

Bruno Monguzzi puts forth work that enlivens and enlightens. His intimate understanding of his discipline has blossomed into an integral entity of form, craft, and function in the service of effective visual communication. To understand Bruno Monguzzi is to know his passion to communicate effectively and gracefully. Firmly rooted in his own time, Monguzzi's designs are nourished by existing elements and a knowledge of history that allows him to integrate the past and present. His fresh interpretations of masters such as Zdanevich, Lissitzky, Zwart, Tschichold, Bayer, Sutnar, and others are unlike the appropriating practices of the past decade, a trend of contemporary misinterpretations of historic material in the guise of "style" or "fashion."

The "returns" of Monguzzi's "consultations" with history are an educated response and a sensitive application of relevant elements. Monguzzi's oeuvre is not unlike the coda of a musical composition, in which ideas expressed earlier are not merely reiterated, but expanded upon and ultimately transformed into something entirely different and yet comprehensive of all preceding references.

Equally significant is that Monguzzi's work has resisted classification. Although his career has developed through the mainstream of modernism and the presence of lesser movements, he has managed to create "a school of which he is the sole protagonist, teacher, pupil, and which could be described as magic functionalism."[1] He extends the vocabulary of twentieth-century design through his mastery as a true poet of form and function — "That appropriate visual forms can arise only in response to careful analysis of a problem is not an obscure idea in the late twentieth-century; however, many lesser designers who purport to practice this concept in actuality bow to the dictates of fashion and produce little more than stylistic affectation — rarely the answer to a client's needs. Bruno Monguzzi, however, consciously and successfully tailors solution to problem.

He is at home with three-dimensional designs for exhibitions as he is with two-dimensional catalogues, posters and printed ephemera, and the entire scope of his work, though broad, reflects his careful consideration of each detail in relation to the desired communication."[2]

The Development of the Designer

Bruno Monguzzi was born on August 21, 1941, at Mendrisio (Ticino) in the picturesque lake region of southern Switzerland. This unique part of the country has been a member of the Swiss Federation for only one hundred and fifty years. It shares a set of values and purpose with the German-speaking Swiss and French-speaking

1. Michel Wassikoff, "Bruno Monguzzi: Exposition à la Maison du Livre de l'image et du son, Villeurbanne," *Signes 7*, 1992, p. 45.
2. Ken Carls, *Contemporary Designers*, London: Macmillan Publishers, 1984, p. 426.

Swiss to the north, east, and west respectively, along with a shared culture with the Italians to the south. The Monguzzi family was made up of his late father, Luigi, mother, Valentina, brother, Giancarlo, and Bruno.

"My father and my mother were very different from each other — they still were two years ago when my father died — and my brother was very different from me. He was good in everything."[3] Luigi, "a small artisan, loved what he did with his hands, with his eyes, with his thought, and he wouldn't stop until he had accomplished perfection."[4] He was a cabinetmaker and restorer of furniture — a craft requiring great patience and talent. Valentina, "had the extraordinary humbleness not to understand, when there was really nothing to be understood."[5] The imprint of a multilingual and multicultural environment provided Monguzzi with a unique view of things together and with a quest for meaning, later to inform and enrich his work. "I grew up — if one can say such a thing — between two conceptions of the world: the proto-liberal-Catholic vision of my mother, and the vetero-social-Marxist credo of my father. I have always remained a permanent child and never ceased asking, Why? An incautious adolescent who dreamed of changing the world — first with a pencil, later through revolution — it was the world, of course, that changed me. But it was in fact due to those interwoven moralisms that the search for meaning became a natural need to me, and that they, my father and my mother, unaware, became my first teachers."[6]

His parents, together with their "interwoven moralisms," were different from each other as are Bruno and Giancarlo, an economist. Monguzzi notes that the "lessons my father gave me without being aware of it seemed right from the beginning obsessed by perfection, in that you are to strive for perfection in whatever it is you are doing, whether it is a tiny little job or very important work. This is probably something that I still have to fight within myself because in some cases, there is no perfection to be reached. It is an endless process."[7] From his mother, he learned the importance of having "everything make sense and be understandable."[8] He remembers both his parents passing on to him an acute sense of duty and an instinctive urge to differentiate between good and evil. As Monguzzi explains, "These two imperatives formed me: everything has to have a reason, everything has to be good for humanity."[9] In sum, Monguzzi seeks to produce stimulating work with the perfectionism of an artisan and with the inclusiveness and universality of his mother's faith.

As a child, Monguzzi was involved in the art of communication in various ways. He enjoyed writing and was a talented child actor, playing parts in both children's and adult theatre for a small local company. He also excelled in gymnastics and longed

3. Bruno Monguzzi, "An Autobiographical Note," *Idea* 267, 1998, p. 80.
4. Ibid.
5. Ibid.
6. Ibid.

7. Bruno Monguzzi, Interviews with Franc Nunoo-Quarcoo, 1998, Meride, Switzerland.
8. Ibid.
9. Monguzzi, "An Autobiographical Note," p. 81.

very much to play the drums. In all of these activities there are shared qualities: dialogue, drama, intonation, sequence, narrative, rhythm, inflection, flexibility, inventiveness, ingenuity, and discipline — qualities that are also essential for effective visual communication. They speak to the universality of communication, spoken, read, touched, or otherwise experienced. Monguzzi excelled in school through passionate application to his studies. He had aspired to be an architect, but was convinced that he had to become an engineer first, and mathematics, a requisite for an engineering degree, was not a favorite subject. Monguzzi then focused his sights on graphic design, which he started studying immediately after obligatory school. At about the age of fifteen, in the mid 1950s, Monguzzi began reading the works of Albert Camus, Simone Weil, Martin Buber, and Jean-Paul Sartre in order to develop an understanding of the whole of things and not merely the singular or the individual. It was such literature that addressed issues of complexity, contradictions, and contrapositions that shaped the beliefs of a generation that had to mature in the shadows of catastrophic human foibles.

Perhaps these issues may help in understanding the paradoxes and contradictions present in Monguzzi's work. The book that marked Monguzzi most deeply as a young man is *Letter to a Teacher* (*Lettera a una Professoressa*), written by a group of fifteen-year-old Italian students as a challenge to state-and church-run schools and institutions in Italy and as a tribute to a teacher, Father Milani. Born to a Jewish mother, Milani entered the Roman Catholic priesthood late in life. He was a vocal critic of the Church and had been banished to a small, rural parish without a school. Nevertheless, he went on to establish a school, and taught, fostering an extraordinary experience with the children of the village, which led to the book. *The Little Prince* by Antoine de Saint-Exupéry is another book fundamental to the shaping of the young Bruno Monguzzi as an adolescent. This book explained to him in metaphor the multiplicity and differences of the peoples of the world. It painted a portrait of and allowed for his discovery of humanity. Monguzzi states that he continued to re-read it, and gained more with each reading.

Moving to Geneva with his family and enrolling in the École des Arts Décoratifs, Monguzzi envisioned graphic design as a form of visual communication — a language and a mode of barrier-free exchange. He had grown up speaking Italian, learned to speak French and German in school, taught himself English, and now surmised that he was about to learn the universal mode of communication. "I attended a Swiss design school, was a diligent student, acquired a good hand, was confronted with a few dogmas and several private gospels, and had to discover, at my own expense, that a graphic design course had little to do with

communication. Most of my 'whys' were unanswered, and for
a kid in search of the universal language this became too
frustrating."[10] His disappointment lay not specifically with the
school he attended, but with the vagueness of the profession
itself. He began to question if graphic designers were "makers of
communication problems or solvers of communication
problems."[11] Being from Ticino, Italian Switzerland, living and
attending school in the Calvinist city of Geneva, in French Switzerland, and receiving a contradictory and stylistic visual education
based on the Swiss School heavily influenced by German Switzerland was perplexing. Although he was attracted to the Swiss
German graphic design culture, he soon realized that even
the Swiss School, the crucible of visual communication, failed to
answer his many questions and queries. His questions during
critiques were an irritation for some teachers. It was never enough
just to know he had made a mistake. He had to understand why.
The graphic design he was being taught had little to do with
communication; instead the focus was on arranging elements on
a surface in order to establish "good" visual relationships with
"good" tensions. As far as narration and understanding the
content, there was a lack of consideration. Many of the solutions
he saw being taught belonged more to a formulaic style than
to a functional approach. What Monguzzi wanted to do was to
learn how to communicate. The experiences of his formative
years, especially living in a multilingual environment as a minority,
had shaped Monguzzi's appreciation for clear and effortless
communication.

During this time, Monguzzi was exposed to the works of Swiss
designers Hans Neuburg, Carlo Vivarelli, and the photographically
dominant work of Josef Müller-Brockmann, which were "just
powerful communication and extremely beautiful design."[12]
Perhaps more important to Monguzzi's education was his discovery of the works of Herbert Bayer, Jan Tschichold, Piet Zwart,
Paul Shuitema, El Lissitzky, and the experiments of the avant-
garde movements, particularly the *X-beelden* and the *Soldaten*
series published by Theo Van Doesburg in *De Stijl*.
His visual communication roots took hold with these masters.
They were fundamental to his education and through them he
understood the "objective" practice of typography that eschewed
dogma. He also understood that objective typography was only
one aspect of the typographic language.

London and the American Masters

Disappointed with his progress at the École des Arts Décoratifs,
he wrapped up his studies in Geneva by combining his final two
years, and at the age of nineteen, he arrived in London on a Swiss
scholarship to pursue studies in typography, photography,

1

2

3

4

10. Ibid.
11. Monguzzi, Interviews with
 Nunoo-Quarcoo.
12. Ibid.

1. Josef Müller-Brockmann
 Watch that Child, poster, 1953.
2. Herbert Bayer
 60th Birthday Exhibition, poster, 1926.
3. Piet Zwart
 Reclame, booklet, 1931.
4. Theo Van Doesburg (J.K. Bonset)
 Soldaten series, De Stijl, IV, 11, 1921.

and the psychology of perception. This was to form the bedrock and focus of his methodology. He became a "free student" by managing to create a colloquium with Dennis Bailey at the London School of Printing, Ken Briggs and Romek Marber at the St. Martin's School, and David Collins at the Central School. The young Monguzzi had assembled a faculty who, he hoped, could answer his many questions about visual communication. His sojourn to London and the collection of instructors established a crucial point in his journey to verify the validity of visual communication as a profession. "It is there, in 1960, that I also began to study the typography of the avant-garde movements of the twenties, and that my eyes began to grasp the meanings beyond the look. It is there that the thick skin of an allegedly brilliant student began to peel off in a slow, long process still in progress. It is surprising how radical the damage of a formalistic education can be. You learn a style and you ignore the message, the scope, the receiver. The umbilical cord that links the eye to the brain, and the brain to the hand may be irreversibly cut then, before you are even born."[13] Monguzzi's search for meaning in visual communication had begun.

London proved to be a positive turn at the fork in the road. His introduction and subsequent exposure to both a new language and culture sharpened his observational and expressive skills. "It is in London, … that I began to make a nondogmatic distinction between objective and expressive typography. Between typography where the formal content fades out to pass on the message as neutrally as possible, and the typography where the formal content affirms itself immediately to predetermine the meaning, or to implement a more specific meaning."[14] Particularly in his relationship with Dennis Bailey and Romek Marber, Monguzzi grew in his understanding of graphic design as a more expressive practice than what he had studied in Switzerland. Ken Briggs introduced him to Gestalt psychology. Monguzzi studied Rudolf Arnheim's *Art and Visual Perception* and Kurt Koffka's *The Principles of Gestalt Psychology*. The key premise for Monguzzi was that the laws of perception are similar for every human mind. Monguzzi began to understand that there is a way to present information that would be "read" and understood simultaneously by different groups of people.

All of his work is based on perceptual laws, which in turn are based on the principles of association: "If you take two very similar elements, and you distance them, they can still be linked if they differ radically from the surrounding elements. What is difficult to foresee is how an individual will implement or complement these perceptual/ structural/ associative laws. Each individual will bring something personal we cannot plan into the equation, and therefore the most important way to communicate is to orchestrate and organize the significant elements on

13. Bruno Monguzzi, Lecture, Icograda Congress, 1995, Lisbon.
14. Bruno Monguzzi, Lecture, AIGA New York, 1987, New York.

a page in a manner that provides fundamental connections that are difficult to be destroyed by personal preferences and interferences."[15] Hence the quality of communication is determined by the quality of the signifiers and their associations. For Monguzzi, the point about these theoretical readings was not to qualify as a psychologist, but rather to learn to look, experiment, and then discover a way to communicate effectively. With this knowledge came a lifelong pursuit of visual education, what he terms "the broadening of the eyes."[16] One communicates effectively by understanding how to construct and by learning how to "read" words and images.

5

Alongside the discovery of Gestalt psychology and visual perception, Monguzzi also encountered the American school of visual communication, the polar opposite of what he had observed in Switzerland as a young student.

6

"It was in London again that, through Karl Gerstner's book *Neue Grafik* and Aaron Burns's *Typography,* I discovered and admired the elegance and the intelligence of a few American designers who were ignored during my Swiss studies because they were too far from the Swiss models: Gene Federico, Lou Dorfsman, Herb Lubalin (I am referring to the first Lubalin, before the sixties), and that, paradoxically, I finally understood a Swiss Master, Karl Gerstner."[17] In the Americans, he found a concern with first developing an intelligent concept and then following with the design. They integrated typography and photography in a much freer way, leading to extremely functional communication. There were no apprehensions about the rules of type, scale, and color to achieve the optimum in visual communication. Their characteristic dramatic uses of body size and variety in typefaces proved that inflection and variation were potent structural elements both to verbal and visual communication.

7

To Monguzzi, the exquisite 1953 "She's got to go out to get *Woman's Day*" magazine double-page advertisement designed by
5   Gene Federico, the advertisements for Sudler, Hennessey &
6   Lubalin advertising by Herb Lubalin, the 1956 "The Light Touch" advertisement about "soft sell" versus "hard sell" in advertising
7   by Lou Danziger, and the 1961 "ha ha ha: He laughs last best who laughs last" advertisement about comedy (showing CBS's
8   domination) by Lou Dorfsman for CBS "were fundamental for my education."[18] Thanks to these Americans Monguzzi realized there was a more sophisticated way to be "objective":
"A typographical designer has to understand that the shape given to a word can be a form of communication, not a form of decoration, and any manipulation of a word enters in fact into the signifying process."[19]

8

40   15. Monguzzi, Interviews with
        Nunoo-Quarcoo.
      16. Ibid.
      17. Monguzzi, Lecture, AIGA New York.
      18. Monguzzi, Interviews with
        Nunoo-Quarcoo.
      19. Ibid.

Perhaps the greatest turning point in Monguzzi's career was his encounter and subsequent relationship with Antonio Boggeri and Studio Boggeri in Milan. It was here that the true maturation of Bruno Monguzzi as a bona fide visual communicator took place. He encountered an environment that tested and melded all his natural and intellectual skills into a potent tool. "It was still in London that, in the second issue of the *Neue Grafik* magazine, I was struck by the works of the Milanese Studio Boggeri, a design office that was run by a musician. I had to meet this man. The day I was twenty (I do not like birthdays), I flew to Milan. The elevator of Piazza Duse 3 was tiny, slow, and shaky. During the long ascent to the fifth floor I felt a bit uneasy. This sensation had to last for the following two years. I had fallen in love with the man, his ideas, the office overlooking the public garden. The first weeks were difficult. I used to work also at home, at night, trying desperately to be good enough to be kept there."[20] Studio Boggeri, before Monguzzi, had been staffed by famed Swiss designers like Max Huber, Carlo Vivarelli, Walter Ballmer, and Aldo Calabresi. While many Swiss designers of his generation looked to German-speaking northern Switzerland to start careers, Monguzzi looked to Italy, a country with which he had a shared language and culture.

From the first day, Boggeri gave him real projects demanding real problem-solving skills. Boggeri chose his staff because he believed in their ability to solve problems swiftly and effectively. He never gave ideas and opinions to his designers; instead he presented the objective and the priorities needed to solve the problems at hand. The designer had the task of figuring out the solution while communicating effectively and artfully. Designers were rarely called into his office except for project reviews and the dispensing of information. One afternoon not long after he started working, Boggeri summoned Monguzzi for a little chat. Not to his surprise, thoughts of impending doom and the "shortest career ever" ran through his mind. Boggeri had sometimes complained about Swiss designers being slow.

For Monguzzi, due to his unfulfilled quest for clarification about graphic design and visual communication, Studio Boggeri represented the last check before deciding whether to pursue another profession. Understandably he was apprehensive about stepping into the "office," but what he heard from Antonio Boggeri was the answer he had been looking for all along. "Lowering his thin face (he was very tall) and lifting his lean, long hands — the most beautiful hands I have ever seen — he began to talk about spider webs, all kinds of spider webs. I thought that this was a strange introduction to fire someone. He went on and on for quite sometime, or at least so it seemed to me, and finally

20. Monguzzi, Lecture, Icograda Congress.

he mentioned that Swiss graphic design was often as perfect as
any spider's web. But often of a useless perfection. The web,
he stated, was useful only when broken by the entangled fly. It was
so that, upon Boggeri's instigation, began for me the slow,
long, difficult hunt, in the sterilized universe of a Swiss education,
for an improbable fly."[21]

"Perfection was not enough. The desterilization of Calvinist
rigor was an additional problem I hadn't anticipated. To the construction of anonymous information, so diligently learned and
pursued, I now had to integrate a need that was alien to me at the
time, the need for the Cassandrian 'spectacle dans la rue' that
Boggeri, a refined man, required at all times."[22]

Working beside the seasoned Aldo Calabresi at Studio Boggeri,
Monguzzi learned quickly and properly, providing exquisite,
meaningful, and lasting solutions to projects that crossed his
table. Calabresi, who is Swiss with family origins from Ticino, had
studied design in Zurich. He was instrumental in the growth
of Monguzzi as a visual communicator, showing him by example
how to weave his very person, culture, and learned principles
to communicate effectively. "Before me, behind very thick lenses
and surrounded by a constant buzz, sat Aldo Calabresi. To my
great admiration and envy, myopic as he was, he was a master
9   of massacring flies. His work sharply marked the fusion of the two
cultures — the Swiss, logical and constructive, and the Italian,
poetic and anarchical. It was primarily because of Aldo that a fly
or two began to buzz in my direction, at last breaking my
painstakingly constructed web. Leaving the shattered grid to
the Freudians, the fly seems to be the identity I have sought in my
work ever since. This identity, perhaps, is innate or ingrained in
this little triangle of Helvetian earth infiltrating the soil of Lombardy, where the people are too Italian to be really Swiss, but too
Swiss to be considered truly Italian."[23]

At the the Aspen Design Conference in 1981, the theme was
"The Italian Idea." As Monguzzi recalls, "Leo Lionni was the
moderator of the panel that was meant to illuminate this rather
obscure topic. Bill Lacy, chairman at the time, had chosen half
a dozen full blooded Italian speakers, but also wanted a couple of
'bastards.' Leo Lionni was actually the first, I was the second.
As a matter of fact most American designers think I am Italian.
Even some Swiss still do. On the contrary Italian designers,
in spite of my Italian name, swear I am 'Svizzero.'
Some time ago I happened to receive a letter from the United
States with a surprising address:

Bruno Monguzzi
6866 Meride
Svizzera
Italy.

9

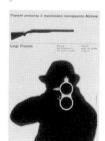

42   21. Ibid.
22. Carls, p. 427.
23. Monguzzi, Lecture, AIGA New York.

Leo Lionni, when introducing himself, admitted that he feels one hundred per cent Dutch, one hundred per cent Italian, and one hundred per cent American. Luckily enough I escaped that question, because on this matter I was, and still am, very confused."[24]

Post Studio Boggeri and North America

At the end of two productive years, Monguzzi developed a confidence that enabled him to move on. He had gained the courage and confidence to spark a discovery and joy for visual communication.

After his tenure at Studio Boggeri, Monguzzi began to teach and work independently in Milan. He designed for IBM and for Gavina, the Italian furniture manufacturer. While printing an IBM catalogue at Fantoni Grafica in Venice, he was asked by the president of the printing firm to teach courses on typographic design at the Cini Foundation in Venice. There began a life-long career as a teacher.

Between teaching jobs at the Cini Foundation, he spent two summers in London working with former professors. The first summer, he worked with Romek Marber on the design of the first issue of an illustrated magazine for the *Observer* newspaper that ushered in the beginning of illustrated supplements for weekend editions of newspapers in Britain. The second summer, he worked with the architect Alan Irvine. They designed exhibitions on art treasures from Romania and town planning for the city of Liverpool.

80

The day before leaving London for Milan, he discovered he had been favorably referred to James Valkus, a New York designer who was embarking on designing pavilions for Montreal's Expo '67 (with the theme Man the Provider) in association with the Montreal design office of Charles Gagnon. Because of his commitments in Italy, Monguzzi hesitated to accept this offer, but when shown the beautiful work of Valkus and Gagnon for the Canadian National Railroad Company, he accepted. His arrival in Montreal in 1965 marked an important point in Monguzzi's career. Working in three dimensions, his principles about structure and perception could now be applied to solving complex and varied problems. In addition, international forums require universal modes of communication. He was contracted to design nine exhibition pavilions, and his organizational, communication, and visual skills would be put to the test. The pavilions were roughly designed before he arrived. Characteristically, he revised proposals and redesigned entire portions of the exhibitions in order to better communicate the intent. All nine pavilions needed to have something to tie them together to communicate that they were related entities.

24. Monguzzi, Lecture, Icograda Congress.

89 In these pavilions, he sought to design an environment where research data would be contextualized to explain and present information to the public. Although not all of his proposals and designs were realized, the young Swiss designer learned much about group dynamics and the politics of realizing a large project. Communication in these situations is an endless maze, and the practice of design is as much affected by cultural and political tendencies as it is by other elements.

After the Montreal Expo '67 project, Monguzzi stayed on to work on proposals for a comprehensive visual identity project for the Metropolitan Transport Authority of New York (Metra). "Metra" was initiated to address the coordination of travel timetables and other pertinent communication matters, with the hope of creating a comprehensive public transportation system not unlike those found in major European cities. Although Monguzzi designed the logo, the project did not proceed past the proposal stage. The Canadian National Film Board (CNFB) was another noteworthy project Monguzzi worked on. It was the national entity for Canada's film industry, but also encompassed other forms of communication. With the then-current name, it failed to communicate effectively because it addressed only one activity and lacked the synthesis of a name and acronym that worked well both in English and French. Before creating the actual design, he analyzed the functions of the Film Board, starting with the name, acronym, and its effectiveness, in all forms. He especially worked on getting the new name, Canadian Communication Centre or Centre de Communication Canadien (CCC) to work on all fronts both in English and French.

A New Beginning

88 Back in Milan, he engaged in a modest graphic identification project for a small, young publishing company. These simple books possessed an elegance and functionality. For his "efforts to make type read,"[25] Monguzzi was honored with the Bodoni Prize in 1971 for " having made a definite contribution to the betterment of Italian graphic design."[26] Critical to Monguzzi's development as an effective designer is that the quality of his solutions has always reflected an acute awareness of the quality of the communication, without regard for the size or importance of the project. The methodology developed earlier in his career had not wavered with the passage of a decade. He was not complicit with the fashion system that championed style for style's sake, disregarded clarity in communication, and misguidedly adopted personalizing information for public dialogue. Because of his nondogmatic manner of approaching communications problems of varied complexity, his output showed a maturity that belied his age.

25. Monguzzi, "An Autobiographical Note," p. 83.
26. Ibid.

Monguzzi had reached a crossroads in life. He had essentially ended his "first life" after his visit to Mexico. He was thirty years old, and he had just begun to "understand life and somehow I felt I did not belong to the profession."[27] He was newly married to the beautiful and sophisticated Milanese Anna Boggeri, daughter of Antonio Boggeri. He sought some removal from a profession he questioned, as he pondered options for a life ahead with a family. Fondly remembering his teaching experience at the Cini Foundation, he contacted Max Huber, the Swiss designer who practiced design and had taught in Milan at the Scuola Unimataria (the Humanitarian School). Huber suggested approaching a new school of design in Lugano, Switzerland. This part of Switzerland is famed as a beautiful resort, but was not then known for fine educational and cultural institutions. To the Lugano School of Design, he proposed a curriculum with a then-radical approach to visual communication. The director, enthusiastic about the young professor and his ideas, secured his services, and the following year Monguzzi was joined by Max Huber.

Bruno Monguzzi had begun a second life: He has been at the Lugano School of Design for over a quarter of a century, attaining a legendary status as a beloved and challenging master teacher. Alberto Bianda, a student from twenty-two years ago, remembers the intensity and purpose of the exercises and projects given by Monguzzi. The emphasis was always on learning how to communicate. Monguzzi's own experiences as a student had prepared his approach to problem-solving methodologies for young designers in their formative years. Bianda recalls that "Monguzzi spoke a language that was very accessible. He taught me how to look and what to look for. I was fascinated by him. He is kind and generous, and it is easy to develop a friendship and a relationship. Our friendship has grown over the years."[28] Now an art director and instructor at the Lugano School of Design alongside his former professor and mentor, Bianda further notes that Monguzzi "is very popular with students. His teaching is involved, practical, and intellectual."[29] Concerning both work and instruction, Bianda points out that "Monguzzi investigates like an engineer and solves like a poet."[30]

Monguzzi reconnected with Studio Boggeri. One project he engaged was the design of an aspect of the Pirelli tire company logo. Pirelli was having difficulty using the lengthy Pirelli logo in a smaller size for product identification and placement.

85   Monguzzi utilized the highly recognizable initial P of Pirelli and hand-constructed a circular version of the P, maintaining a visual link between the new form and the existing element. At once the circular shape addressed a tire, and the bent shape exemplifies the pliable qualities of rubber.

The name Roberto Sambonet also occupies an important part of Monguzzi's design oeuvre. Sambonet, Monguzzi, and the

27. Monguzzi, Interviews with
   Nunoo-Quarcoo.
28. Alberto Bianda, Unpublished interview
   with Franc Nunoo-Quarcoo,
   June 6, 1998, Meride, Switzerland.
29. Ibid.
30. Ibid.

architect Giancarlo Ortelli established a productive and artful

90 working relationship. For several years, they designed exhibitions,

93 environmental graphic design, and packaging. One of Monguzzi's most talked about collaborations is *Della Pazzia (*1977*)*, an album of drawings of inmates in a Brazilian mental institution. The drawings, showing the many faces of insanity, by Sambonet, were printed as part one of a two-section presentation.

101 *Della Pazzia* part two, composed by Monguzzi, portrays insanity as found in literature and music. This extraordinary document is eloquently described by both Hans Christian Besemer and Gene Federico. The powerful design of *Della Pazzia* was important in Monguzzi's induction into the Alliance Graphique Internationale (AGI), a collection of the world's eminent design practitioners. In 1979 a modest Monguzzi reluctantly accepted an invitation from Sambonet to attend the AGI Congress in Bath, England, as a guest of the Italian contingent. Sambonet's strong belief in Monguzzi's work was confirmed by those at the Congress who saw Monguzzi's work. He was finally able to meet one of his American masters, the "fantastic communicators,"[31] Gene Federico, and an immediate life-long friendship was established. A couple of years later at an AGI Student Seminar at the State University of New York, Purchase, he met Lou Danziger, another of his American masters. These were the people who "opened my eyes not to graphic design but to visual communication."[32] But, even though he began to garner international recognition for his work, Monguzzi still saw himself as an outsider to the professional practice of design. In *Contemporary Designers*, art historian Ken Carls writes, "By his own admission, Monguzzi is an outsider among his peers in the design field. He welcomes the role of intermediary in the process of public communication. In exercising this role, he insists on selecting appropriate tools to fulfill the criteria of a problem and generally operates intentionally outside the stifling confines of current trends."[33]

Museo Cantonale d'Arte

Of Monguzzi's oeuvre, perhaps the most recognized is the graphic identity and visual communications work for the Museo Cantonale d'Arte in Lugano. Rationalism and poetry are crucial elements of the work. For a large number of his critics, sympathetic or otherwise, he has perfected a rigorous methodology, not a style, whose hallmark is true visual communication. By temperament, Monguzzi is a Cartesian: logical reasoning is the framework, the foundation is the objective of all his enterprises, and in his hands intuition and constructive play are the favored instruments that aid him in defining his perspective in addressing a problem. The humanitarian logic of his perspective on effective

46 31. Monguzzi, Interviews with Franc
Nunoo-Quarcoo.
32. Ibid.
33. Carls, p. 428.

visual communication fully develops around the work he continues to generate for the Museo Cantonale d'Arte.

The Museo Cantonale d'Arte, established in 1987 in the center of the city of Lugano, is the federal cultural museum for the Ticino region of Switzerland.

As part of the Department of Culture and Education, the museum is charged with the cultural enrichment of the people in that region. Manuela Kahn-Rossi, the conservator of the museum, was impressed with the vitality of the Musée d'Orsay program Monguzzi had designed for the Paris museum. Right from the beginning she wanted Monguzzi to be the sole designer of all visual communications for the Museo Cantonale d'Arte. Her brief was complex and daring. First, she wanted the Museo Cantonale d'Arte to have a face, to be recognized as a museum, so she assigned him the task of designing a logo or mark. Second, she wanted the Museo Cantonale d'Arte to have a voice, so she wanted a different poster for every exhibition. For her museum's voice in the public, Kahn-Rossi wanted a visual communication that translated the quality that art has in the domain of the museum. She wanted to capture the essence, the spirit of the exhibits on the posters to the public.

Monguzzi's extensive knowledge of the history of art and design has served him in analyzing difficult assignments. The museum's interests represent an historical span from the nineteenth century into the twentieth, including contemporary art. Monguzzi had to integrate the logo into the voice of the museum, reflecting the museum's commitment to visual communications, which lies in the simple premise to inform, educate, and document its activities for its public, and to provide a visual record for posterity. The depth, meaning, and fruitful collaboration between Monguzzi and the Museo Cantonale d'Arte is best exemplified in the following appreciation by Marco Franciolli, the curator of the museum: "The relationship. Maybe this is the most precious part of it. With Bruno it is a real partnership. Once you accept to work with him, he will not just accept to elaborate an image, he will ask a lot of questions in order to learn and then express your ideas visually. There must be a collaboration between curator and designer, which in my experience is the only way to achieve good results. I think it is extraordinary the way he gives of himself. Not many designers are able to accept criticism and then go back to the beginning and develop another approach. This is something very precious. I think that once someone is really good in his work and he doesn't have to prove anything anymore, he has this privilege to be really modest, and from the human side it is a very nice place to be. This is a quality I very much admire in Bruno. You can have a dialogue even if he is Bruno Monguzzi. He is very secure. He is always excited to design the next poster. I am sure Bruno wouldn't accept to work with the museum anymore if we were to change our line in a direction to which he could not agree. He is able to invest so much in us because the museum's ideas and directions and his are parallel. That is why we decided not to split the work between different designers. The visual identity of the museum is very important, and we have the best in Bruno Monguzzi. After a decade of working together, we are the proud beneficiaries of his exceptional work and vision.

"Last year, to celebrate the museum's tenth anniversary, we celebrated Bruno's activities for the museum with an exhibition of every visual communication he had made for us. In total, he had made a link between all our activities. It was really impressive going into the rooms and seeing the volume of work he had done for us over ten years. It was simply beautiful. Also the choice to show the entire works was to present the museum's collective work of ten years to our public. In this we could also see the construction of our visual identity."[34]

This decade-long collaboration demonstrates that the methodology employed by Monguzzi in planning each design program reveals the common denominator of all the work: the search for a sense, an aspect, that unites results that may vary greatly in appearance. Every featured painter, sculptor, architect, or photographer retains a strong essence and identity regardless of whether their work is reproduced on the posters, book covers, invitations, or brochures. Often only their name appears, but they stand out through references to signifiers that catch the eye, sometimes without any need of familiarity with the work.

For this museum, Monguzzi has adopted this unique approach: the signs and elements he identifies in a project as a whole are not to form a sum, but rather to reinforce one another in directing and enriching the senses. Although every single element is a complete autonomous design, the collective whole is a deft and erudite composition. In all his work for the museum, one is certain not to encounter any evident repetitions from catalogues to invitations to brochures to posters, but rather references inspired by the relationships in the field of visual arts that by structure and analogy enable one to identify the continuity.

The essence of the artist Odilon Redon is revealed in a poster, even if the visual communication is purely typographic; the sheer

132 volume of the typography "Botta" reflects the essential characteristics the architect's church exhibited; and we can imagine

113 Sophie Tauber-Arp turning out eloquently composed paintings with a sophisticated language based on simple forms reminiscent of both the de Stijl and Bauhaus movements. The commitment between the Museo Cantonale d'Arte and Bruno Monguzzi to communicate effectively with the public has borne a breathtaking reference of visual communications and signifies a distinct redefinition of the genre for public and private institutions worldwide.

48 34. Marco Franciolli, Unpublished interview with Franc Nunoo-Quarcoo, June 8, 1998, Lugano, Switzerland.

Bruno Monguzzi's search for meaning is not over.
Like Antonio Boggeri before him, perfection is never enough.
He is often reflective and introspective. From an unpublished
conversation with Antonio Boggeri shortly before Boggeri's
death in 1989, Monguzzi notes, "I often feel responsible, but I only
feel responsible for the mistakes I have made. For the rest,
it has happened the way it was bound to happen. As an inevitable
consequence of the design act."[35]

Of his work and methodology Monguzzi imparts:
"To what extent can a typographic line be objective?
To what extent are these works objective?
Or to what extent are these works subjective?
I frankly do not know.
But I truly hope they are pertinent.
I hope they are intelligent and therefore intelligible,
provocative, and memorable."[36]

35. Antonio Boggeri, Unpublished
    interview with Bruno Monguzzi, 1989.
36. Monguzzi, Lecture, Icograda Congress.

Franc Nunoo-Quarcoo

Creating the Poetry of Form and Function:
A Discussion with Bruno Monguzzi

The interview that follows is a greatly expanded version of one that appeared in *Word+Image: Swiss Poster Design, 1955-1997.*

What is your definition of design?

> The intellectual and pragmatic process aimed at giving an
> appropriate form to a given function.

And what is your definition of typography?

> Typographic design is simply the vehicle through which words
> can be seen, read, and understood. Hopefully. And possibly
> memorized. This is what I had answered a couple of years ago to
> the editor of the *Idea* magazine special issue on typography.
> Ten years ago, for Ruedi Rüegg's *Basic Typography: Design with
> Letters*, I had quoted Lissitzky: "Typographical design should
> perform optically what the speaker creates through voice
> and gesture for his thoughts,"[1] mentioning that this assimilation
> of the work of the typographer with that of the orator seemed to
> me the most relevant and intelligent provocation for young
> students, often sidetracked in the maze of fashion beyond the
> confines of communication. Some people think there is only one
> way to do typography. And this "way," in order to have a "proper"
> personality, has to conform to a given "style" that design critics
> will eventually label, possibly in one or two words. The problem
> arises when the spectrum of the communication is wider than the
> eye of the needle.

The basic elements of visual communication are Word and Image.
Could you describe your thoughts and approach to
the use of typography and photography/illustration in your work?

> Words and images are means, and the means are instrumental for
> the attainment of the scope. What I question first is the relevance
> of the signifier I am planning to use, word or image that it may be.
> I do not see much sense or value in the aesthetic efforts that are
> not pertaining to the message and that often conform to a precon-
> ceived syntax, most commonly a reiteration of the current trend.

Ought the final product to bear the trademark of the designer?

> The communication product should primarily bear the trademark
> of the sender, not the designer. In a way, I liken our role to the role
> of the translator, or as Lissitzky did in 1924, to that of the actor.
> Of course the actor has a voice and a body, but he lends them to
> the character to which he is giving life.

Ought form to derive from the analysis of function?

> Yes. In visual communication, form should be derived from the
> content and the scope of the message. I suppose this is what you

1. Sophie Lissitzky-Kuppers, *El Lissitzky*,
Dresden: Veb Verlag der Kunst, 1967,
pp. 330-64.

mean when you mention the analysis of function. This way
of being "dependent" is a very productive attitude. It leads you to
"independent" answers. Independent from the prefabricated
solutions box.

Is design a discipline that should concern itself with problem-
solving and/or style?

Naturally design is a discipline concerned with problem-solving.
Style, in our case, has to do with the quality of the communication
resulting from a particular use of the linguistic devices.
So the double question is pleonastic; style is implicit, the *how*
defines the *what*.

Is design an expression of art?
Is there a relationship between design and art?
Is design a craft for industrial purposes?

Yes, design is "in fact" a craft for industrial purpose. Whether
it has a relationship with art or not is difficult to say since the term
"art" does not seem to have a univocal meaning. In Italian, for
example, when we talk about "l'arte del comunicare," we simply
refer to the capacity of achieving effective communication,
which I admit, is not very common, but whether it is art or not,
I would not know.

Can the computer substitute for the designer?

It is the nature of any tool to substitute something or someone in
some way, but it always takes a human decision to make the tool
do what it can do in the way it is supposed to do it. It seems,
though, that many graphic designers feel compelled to demon-
strate the fantastic range of possibilities of the tool. When Zwart
1   designed his beautiful page covered with all kinds of typefaces
in all possible body sizes, the only line that was readable read:
"A small selection from our type collection."[2]

What is the role of the computer in the design process?

The computer is a tool. From a critical standpoint, I am somehow
surprised at the interest that this machine has generated.
Before, we never talked about tools, you know, for years and years,
no one fussed much about tools. Now that there is a new one,
it seems that the tool is more important than the artifact and its
message. Compared to previous tools, the computer, as a single
tool, is able to do many more things, faster. It would be like having
a hammer that has at the back of the handle a pair of scissors
and on the tip of the scissors a screwdriver and on the side of the

1

2. Piet Zwart's design was a page for
     the Trio catalogue. Trio was a printer
     in The Hague.

screwdriver a saw, the bottom half for sawing metal and the top half for cutting bread and spreading butter before going to work.

So the fantastic thing about the computer is that you can do so many things just by sitting at your table with five or ten fingers. It's a fantastic tool and that's it. It is as stupid or as intelligent, it is as appropriate or as inappropriate, as the designer that is sitting in front of it. And as vulnerable. It may get a virus or even enter into a coma due to an instant electrical failure.

Has the computer affected your design process?

I could say yes and no. So I have to explain.

I could say no, it hasn't changed because I think the design process is based on methodology, and methodology is nourished by concrete possibilities.

Any tool is implemented into the design process, but I have to decide which tool is appropriate.

I could say yes, because any tool determines some kind of constraint, and the constraints, in fact, determine the rules of the game.

Is there a design ethic?

I would say instead, a designer's ethic.

Our personal beliefs define our personal values, and these values determine our behavior. I should answer, since I am talking to a designer, that these values "design" the way we design. In any case we are confronted with a three-fold responsibility: towards the client, towards the receiver, and towards the environment.

The answer you gave to Valentina Boffa in the *Eye* interview about ethical choices is intriguing. I will be more direct. What do you think about advertising?

"Advertising, in the best of all possible cases, is a thesis sustained by proof and carried along in a suggestive way. In the worst case, it is a legal form of fraud. There are innumerable shades of gray between these two extremes…

I wouldn't lament the fact that in another economic system, advertising would become superfluous…. Even then, there would be enough work for us. Almost every schoolbook is typographically poor; typography and photography are educational methods which are more important than people care to recognize. In fact, proper arrangement of text and the accentuation of its internal structure through the use of typography would be very important for educational books."[3]

This is what Piet Zwart answered in 1934. May I steal his answer?

3. J. Kasander, "Fotografie, tipografie, reclame/Gesprek met architect Piet Zwart," *Contact* 11, 1934, pp. 525-26.

Of course. Although he quickly changed to the subject
of educational books.

> And so do I. I do not want to be dragged down into the moralistic
> war between advertising being "evil" and graphic design being
> "holy." At the new professional university that we are developing
> in Ticino, I am giving priority to didactic communication by asso-
> ciating our school with the local institute that trains teachers.
> This is not because I have something against advertising; good
> products, of course, deserve good communication. It has to
> do with choosing to face the real, actual, and meaningful problems
> with which education is confronted at all levels, and to have
> real factual control over the attempted answers through testing
> by the actual users in the classrooms. Finally, it is also a way
> to escape the waste of so much energy in so many design schools.

What is your design process? Does it follow a particular
or specific set of steps? What happens from beginning to end?

> When I am dealing with a graphic design problem, the process is
> simply the communication process.
> a. whom; b. what; c. how.
> a. To whom are you talking?
> Who is your audience?
> b. What do you have to say?
> Communication is ultimately dealing with what you wish to
> happen in someone else's mind. So, what kind of response are you
> trying to achieve? And, or, what kind of information do you need
> to pass on?
> c. And which are the appropriate devices?
> And how do you have to organize them in order to achieve this
> scope?
> These are the steps.

Can you think of a project that exemplifies your process?

142 Let's take *Fragile*, a poster for a collective travelling exhibition of
eighteen young artists from three countries: Switzerland, France,
and England. These artists, all very different from one another,
were selected because they all are, in some respect, marginal
figures. Additionally, they are peripheral even within their
own countries. So, to come back to the process, the public I'm
addressing has some cultivation, curiosity, and an interest
in art. What I want to do is to intrigue, to provoke, and to inform.
The devices I have used are: the large stencil lettering obviously
related to the term "fragile" and to travelling; the introduction
of the marks GB, F, and CH, which stand for Great Britain, France,
and Confederatio Helvetica, which means Switzerland.

This was meant to immediately communicate the international scope of the exhibition. The last device was to lay all the type around the periphery, an allusion to the marginality of the artists. This makes an almost empty poster with a lot of white space in the middle, a small provocative introduction to the eighteen provocations that you will be confronted with if you go to see the exhibition.

Weren't you afraid someone would use this empty space?

In fact, this is what Anna said when she saw the final project. I told her I didn't really mind if this would happen. I would see it as a kind of further promulgation of the spirit of the exhibition in the street. The evening of the opening, when the posters had been in the street for five days, one of the artists told me that on the way to the museum, he had seen a *Fragile* poster with a large handwritten word on it. I said that one could expect this to happen. "Guess what they wrote?" he asked. I had no idea. "Bello," he said. And he seemed pleased.

Marco Franciolli mentioned that you had other solutions.

Usually, I do not stop at the first idea. I try to consider different possibilities, and most of the time I have enough information to decide on my own. I often push different solutions to an advanced stage, and then make a choice. In some cases, I take the different proposals to the museum. In this case, I was explained the philosophy of the collective exhibition and was introduced to the work of some of the artists by general descriptions. When I actually started to work on the poster, Marco had slides of only a few of the eighteen artists. So I didn't have a clear vision of what the exhibition was going to look like. I therefore started in different directions, ending up with one idea based solely on text, and two photographic concepts. I made a little sketch of the typography as one solution and a small drawing for the first photographic solution. I was planning to use just an egg: a huge egg to be suggested by a little bit of shadow on the right side of the egg and a little bit of gray background defining its left side. The idea was to have your brain build up the egg out of two little areas, which was a concept of fragility. Because of the subject, and because of the perceptual ambiguity.

2   For the third idea, I built the setting on my table using my drawing lamp to cast the broken shadow of an egg across the mirror on which the egg was only partially sitting; the mirror therefore also breaking the egg's reflection. The names of the artists would lay on a white sheet of paper laid over the mirror, to form a scalene triangle to oppose the circular trilogy of the egg, its shadow, and its reflection. The title "Fragile" would be a reflected image in

2

connection with the broken, mirrored image of the egg. I made
a Polaroid, but it was so bad that I asked the curator to come over.
I had not enough elements to decide myself which approach
would be worth carrying on.

Marco immediately rejected the first egg because its strong conceptual approach would not be a good introduction to the
exhibit. Having now seen the exhibition, I think he was quite right.
He liked very much the second photographic approach, but again,
was afraid that the poster would be too sophisticated.

And again, he was quite right. He picked the typographical solution, the most direct, finding the use of stencil and the addition of
CH, F, and GB very appropriate.

Are you a designer who reads and intervenes in the text?

I find I can't work with a nonconvincing copy or a nonconvincing
brief. With Roberto Sambonet, besides writing the title for the
95 exhibition *Processo per il Museo-Brera*, which literally translates
"Trial for the Brera Museum," we encouraged Franco Russoli
(the museum director) to shut down the rest of the museum,
as a protest against the Rome bureaucracy. This was, of course,
illegal, but he did it anyway. The exhibition truly became an act
of denunciation, provoking the great stir in the press that Russoli
had been expecting for years.

Could you tell me about the big X?

The big X comes from the word "per," the key word in the title.
In Italian, as I said, it means "for." But it is also the symbol
for multiplication. Which in its turn, has also another meaning,
a universal one. It negates what's underneath: in this case,
the physical decay of the museum.

A semantic "tour de force."

I also rewrote some of the exhibit titles. To achieve better clarity
and to gain conceptual and formal strength, I made the titles of
the four introductory exhibitions begin with "Brera": *Brera Today,*
Brera and the City, Brera and Society, Brera and History.

The way you laid out the small text is quite effective. Did you start
from the sad hanging bulb? And what about the photo? Did you
find it, or was it shot specifically for the poster?

I started from the central axis established by the vault, by the X,
and by the sad hanging bulb, as you appropriately named it. I used
the opposing orientations of the arms of the X to distinguish the
two parts of the exhibition that were actually located to the right

3

and to the left of the entrance. So I didn't really invent anything. Conceptually, it is the plan of the exhibition.

3   About the photo, you have to know that the existing poster for the Pinacoteca di Brera that had been around for several years showed a detail from Piero della Francesca's last masterpiece, commonly known in Italy as *La Madonna dell'Ovo.* The egg is hanging from the famous vault in the shape of a shell. The analogy is astounding. You can imagine me when I saw the hanging bulb in the contact sheets I was going through to select the images for the *Brera Today* introduction.
The poster was done. I was very lucky. I am often lucky. I find things. I often use elements that are already there. I just combine them and let them talk.

You search for clues in anticipation of possible solutions to problems, like you did in the Mola triptych. But tell me first about the triptych idea. How did it originate?

When the Museo Cantonale d'Arte was going to open, Manuela Kahn, the director, wanting a strong visibility in the streets, decided for a massive poster campaign, including the F4 and the F12 sizes.[4] For some reason, I did not like the idea of designing and printing a vertical and a horizontal version of the same poster. It seemed to me more reasonable to use the F4 poster also in the F12 format, and to develop complementary roles for the remaining two posters. Since Manuela had stubbornly wanted a logo for the museum, in order to introduce the logo, I made it gigantic.

109   The poster was nearly filled. Just enough space was left for the name of the museum on one side, and the title of the first exhibition, *Il Ticino nella pittura europea* (The Ticino Landscape in European Painting) on the other. I decided to flank the typographical poster with a close-up of a portrait from the museum's permanent collection, and a detail of a landscape from the exhibition. Since the production of the posters was supported by a private foundation, I was able to select three different works from the museum collection and three more from the exhibition. They could be freely interchanged in the street and sold independently in the museum. A didactic note about the artist, a second note about the painting, and a small reproduction of the total work, were printed on the back of each poster.

By revealing its assemblage, you created an open system.

I like your definition of "open system." I like open systems. I like complex systems — not complicated systems — because they prevent too much repetition. As a matter of fact, the two remaining posters can still be used as a linear continuation of the

122   first. Like I did in the Melotti poster. Or as an "introduction"

4. Posters in Switzerland are governed by a standardized system of sizes. The smaller and the most diffuse are the F4 (128 x 90.5 cm.) and the F12 (128 x 271.5 cm.). The F4 is vertical, while the F12 is horizontal. The F12 is formed by three F4s, put together with one centimeter overlaps.

136 to the last, like I did with Kandinsky. The paper joints are, in these
cases, not expressed, giving a single large horizontal image.
Independent statements can precede the informational poster;
114 they can also follow it, as in the Flammer/Paolucci exhibition;
135 or they can flank it, as in Corot, where, having only a few spaces
for triptychs, I simply silkscreened flat fields of color — which
is very economical — to build the French flag. Or, again the same
130 trick, in the case of the Panza di Biumo collection, where the
yellow echoes the flat yellow of the room *Song of No Mind* by Allan
Graham and the blue echoes the blue of *Blue Oval* by Robert
Therrien, two complementary works that were facing each other
in the exhibition.

You manage to turn limitations into possibilities.

Walter Binder, the curator of the Swiss Foundation for Photography in Zürich, asked me to design the poster for an historical
exhibition about photographers from Ticino. It was the first time
he contacted me, and he immediately mentioned that the
Foundation had very little money. Manuela Kahn, with whom
I had just started working, told me that the winter exhibition
was going to be on photography. When I realized that it was the
same exhibition, I proposed to both to make only one poster.
They would save money on the project and the printing. Since
photography is "double" — positive/negative, light/shadow — it
3 was reasonable to split the poster in half. In Zurich, they would
110 just hang it upside down.

The old lady holding the missal in one hand and a faded white rose
in the other, as opposed to Gerevini's flash of white flame is
shocking. But I would like to come back to the Mola triptych we
were discussing earlier.

Yes, here too, I was pretty lucky.
When Manuela first introduced me to the Mola exhibition,
I realized that the museum would be occupied almost in its
entirety. Only a separate elongated room in the oldest wing of the
museum would be left free. Was it possible, was it meaningful
to reduce the collection to that extreme? We decided to juxtapose
a small exhibition of the twentieth-century masters from the
museum collection to the Mola exhibition.
Before leaving, Manuela asked me to investigate the possibility
of using a detail of Mola's *Oriental Warrior*, a fundamental piece
she was going to get from the Louvre. Although the use of details
was not a rigid rule, she had found intriguing the few extreme
croppings I had previously attempted. I took home a postcard of
the *Warrior,* laid over it an A4 acetate with a fine, scratched
diagonal, and discovered that the painting had exactly the same

proportion as the poster. I could use it in its entirety. I did not start cropping. I would decide later with a twentieth-century master work in my hands.

I looked through the entire museum, but nothing struck me.

So the following week I went slowly through the museum storage rooms with the *Warrior* in my mind, and the postcard in my pocket. When *Pathos* by Klee appeared, I was bewildered. I kept staring at it. I couldn't believe it. I finally took the card out. They were

116 identical. Then the connecting game started.

I can see Baroque reminiscences in the typeface you chose for Mola; I can even find a subtle structural analogy between the ornate capital letter M and the gesture of the warrior.

The chromatic relationships are also evident. Could you tell me how you started?

Considering the structural affinity of the two works of art, I knew I had to set them apart. And considering their structural complexity, I knew that a simple and strong connecting element would enhance their different pictorial and chromatic qualities. Black seemed inevitable.

To contrast the italic type and the complexity of the two works of art, I played around with orthogonal plane figures. Satisfactory in the triptych version, they all failed when viewed as a single poster. A stronger allusion to Baroque was needed.

I restarted with the shape of the articulated stucco frame of a Mola fresco: *Padre Eterno Benedicente* from the vault of the Colderio Madonna del Carmelo, a church I knew from my childhood. A central square, linked at the top and at the bottom with two smaller lunettes. I focused on the conjunction of the square with the lower lunette. A right angle and a circle. This gave me the synthesis I needed.

I now needed the fly to fly in, the abrupt diagonal stroke to dialogue with the bowstring and the arrow on one side, and with the many straight strokes of the brush on the other. Just as the impending curve does with the bow, with the double fold in the dress between the warrior's legs, and with the alternatingly suffering, gentle, or powerful bending strokes of Klee's brush.

And the connecting game went on.

The search for connection is also evident in the Flammer/Paolucci triptych.

All the elements seem interwoven in an inextricable way.

114 Again, I started with the selection of two significant works that would stand the bustle of the street. The works I used bear in common the strong verticality of their structure. But at the same time, they are totally opposed: dark vs. light, and full vs. empty.

I therefore chose two opposed symbolic figures to become
the skeleton of the informational poster.
The blue disk was originated by Paolucci's sky blue amoeba.
The black rectangle was in connection with Flammer's
photographic work based on the ancient Egyptian *Book of the
Dead*. Under each photograph Flammer handwrote the quote from
the *Book of the Dead* that had guided him. The twenty-two photographs were exhibited in a painted black oval space I had
designed to avoid corners in the development of the narration.
The strokes of light over the Egyptian columns and the slender-
ness of Paolucci's *Object* generated the vertical bars containing
the names of the artists. To weaken their integration with the
superimposed symbolic figures, and to strengthen the allusion
to a stroke of light, I softened the right and left sides of each
bar by screening the edges.
At this point, I was compelled to perpetrate a typographical
capital sin: setting the fourteen letters of each name, one letter
under the other. But, I must admit, my Swiss side is still recal-
citrant. All the texts could only quietly run along the top.
With five contrapuntistic black bars to structure the information.

I can see you love music. But let's talk more about typography.
The recalcitrance you mention does not really show in your work.
You seem to shift with graceful nonchalance from strict
typographical orthodoxy to total anarchy.

From Bakunin to Calvin. That's nice, as long as it isn't a one-way
journey. For different reasons, I like them both, but this is not
the point. In my work with the museum, I am asked to jump
through history. And sometimes I do not even know if I like, as
Bruno, what I find correct as Monguzzi.
My methodology remains the same. If the problems differ, the
answers are naturally bound to change. I look into a problem,
searching for its core, its specificity. It is from this specificity that
the answer is generated.

Can you give an example?

4   In the case of *Itinerari sublimi* [5] — an exhibition of landscapes from
the eighteenth and nineteenth centuries — I used the surface as
a territory and dislocated the five syllables of "I-ti-ne-ra-ri" along
an imaginary journey. This is an obvious visual translation of
the title's meaning. It makes your eye travel. The "ne," located at
the top of the poster, was torn in order to reveal the second "ne,"
set in Fraktur, [6] in opposition to the three Roman neoclassical
faces I used below. A second reading was therefore proposed,
alluding to the crossing of the cultures — the German to the north
and the Latin to the south. The tear being a metaphor of the Alps

4

62   5. *Sublime Itineraries: Travels by Artists,
1750-1850*. The area covered by the
exhibition goes from the southern tip of
the Lake of Lucerne, just north of the
Alps, to the Lakes Region of northern
Italy.

6. Typical German typeface of general
use in northern Switzerland until the
end of the nineteenth century.

as a cultural barrier. A selective reading, based on knowledge
and visual sensitivity. Sensitivity and culture that I always solicit
from the receiver when I am communicating art.
To sublimate "sublimi," I picked a nineteenth-century italic face
used by elegant lithographers and engravers. I was even lucky
enough to find caps with arrows. But with a hyperbolic title and
the exuberance of the historical references, this seemed still
too plain. So I doubled the title into a Baroque double-colored path.

How did you do it?

I wanted the lettering to actually go through a true uneven
movement. I made several attempts by moving the two words on
the glass of the photocopier as it was copying.
Chance is often better than Monguzzi is. But I still had to make
the final choice.

In the case of the Melotti poster, you also doubled the title.
What made you repeat Melotti's name in such a rigorous play
of the opposites: positive vs. negative, bold vs. light,
extended vs. compressed, uppercase vs. lowercase letters?

122   The two Melotti logos were designed to evoke the radical change
that occurred in his sculptural work. Melotti sculptures up to 1937
were elementary and were constructed according to simple
geometric grids or based on primary volumes. When he goes back
to sculpture at the end of the fifties, he begins to use thin steel
rods and metallic gauze. The elements he playfully assembles are
often so light that the sculpture becomes kinetic. I tried to suggest
this kinetic quality with the introduction of the silver background.
The relationship between the two logos keeps changing as you
move along, causing a constant shift in the tonal hierarchies.

5   The square grid of the first logo, inspired by the 1935 *Scultura n. 21*,
tightly holds the second logo and continues in the lower half
of the poster, integrating the typographical play of dates and timetables. Actually, the total triptych is constructed on a very simple
square grid. The height of the poster determines the side of
the square portrait, facing and located to the right, and the height
of the rectangle, formed by two squares that contain the
sculpture in the center of the tryptich. The same rectangle, lying
horizontally in the upper left, contains the logos and the two titles.

In your design of the logo for the Museo Cantonale d'Arte, you
seem to have given consideration to the span of historical time
and evolution as well.

Yes. The three basic shapes, commonly recognized as the fundamental shapes in form making — the circle, the triangle, and

5

the square — were related to the acronym MCA and to the historical span of the museum's collection, from nineteenth century to contemporary art.

I designed a neoclassical Bodoni capital letter A to contain a rationalistic M, based on a square grid alphabet developed by Theo van Doesburg around 1920. I wanted a visually complex mark to express the complexity of art evolution across the turn of the century. The third element was originally a C in the form of a spiral. I tried several simpler C forms, but the logo still looked complicated instead of complex. The absoluteness of the perfect circle finally expressed the historical trilogy.

Let's come back to typographical concepts.

130 The simplest in visual terms, but perhaps the most intriguing, is in relation to the exhibition *The Eighties and Nineties from the Panza di Biumo Collection.* Since the collection was dealing with minimal and conceptual art, I asked myself how I could make the number eighty and the number ninety become minimal, and at the same time be conceptual.

A minimal approach could have been to use only one zero, since it is common to both numbers. And a minimalistic zero is a circle. This seemed visually very strong. I looked again into the number eighty and the number ninety from a conceptual standpoint. We were in 1992.

The eighties had completed their cycle. The nineties were opening a new one. The answer was in the zero.

I now had a visible concept. I sandwiched the two.

Of course, there are cases where the concept can be relayed more directly, or even cases where typography becomes the direct visualization of the text.

Can you think of a couple of cases?

97 In the catalogue for the *Italienisches Möbel Design* exhibition in Cologne, the title was *Entwurf, Gegenstand, Bild.*
"Entwurf" means project. (2D)
"Gegenstand" means object. (3D)
"Bild" means image. (2D)
Beginning on the spine and bending around onto the cover actually made *Gegenstand* three dimensional.

6 *Gamma Film* was very easy.
You have four letters that do not repeat: g, f, i, l.
One letter repeats twice: a.
One letter repeats three times: m.
I made "visible" the repetition of the m.
What else could I do?

6

I picked Franklin Gothic because of the rounded g. The lack of verticality would keep it from competing with "film" and with the reiterated "m"; its distinctiveness from the other letters would also strengthen the reading starting point. And I was lucky enough that "gam" was wider than "film."
I could, therefore, reiterate the whole thing further. Endlessly.
I was afraid Boggeri would find it too obvious. "It's obvious, but not 'too obvious,'" was his verdict. The "a" on the right had saved me.

Another example — in this case I literally followed the text — is a page from the Arti Grafiche Nidasio series.[7]

103 The text reads: "Circumlocution, much in use in political language, in literary language, in juridical language, is the circle of words with which one wishes… ," and the explanation goes on to give an example for each case, concluding that "if circumlocution in these cases can be a useful artifice… in practical language, it can be risky." It is in collaboration with the words "è il giro" (it is the circle) that the large typographical circle builds up.

In a conversation, Anna told me that, not being happy with the results of a professional photographer, you reshot the whole thing in your house, improvising a photographic studio with drafting and bedside lamps. Yet it is a photographic and layout lesson.
I am intrigued by how you placed the pill in respect to the package and to the glass, the progression of the three perfect circles, the pill, the logo, the typographic circumlocution. And the diagonal of the spoon that brings you back to the pill.
But what does the aspirin have to do with circumlocution?

Aside from being circular itself, you discover the answer at the very end of the text, in the last example, a comparative example, that refers to the practical language.
It is the story of Maria's husband who, through a ridiculous circumlocution, manages to fill fourteen lines of text instead of three: "Maria, give me an aspirin. I have a headache."

Here too, on the Nidasio cover, you felt the need for a juxtaposition.

102 Yes. A flat black logo and a white bent logo.
Because they were letterpress printers — an activity still important for them at the time — and lithographic printers.
I shot the white logo on a large cardboard tube to fake a lithographic cylinder. When I don't need four-by-five-inch negatives, I often prefer to do my own photography.

There is always a sense of rightness, a lack of affectation in your work. In some cases, even a disarming directness. How do you apply these qualities?

7. The Milanese printing firm Nidasio had asked Monguzzi for an idea for a form of promotion that would not be seen as an advertisement. With a young copywriter, Monguzzi invented an alphabet book with only one word for each letter. Each word had to bear some sort of connection with communication. Only a few pages got to the final stage, and the collection was never printed.

When you have a problem, the right solution always seems inevitable. The problem is to know what the problem is. Asking the right questions is more difficult than finding the right answers.

85 When I bent the Pirelli P, I thought this was the only possible thing to do.
They already had a logo and wanted a trademark.
What is the best possible relationship between the existing logo and the second device?
What should it say?

8

8 Since "Quotidiano" means "daily," I suggested to rename it, everyday, with the date of that day.
"Quotidiano del 19 Gennaio '88, Quotidiano del 20…, Quotidiano del 21…."
And since the nineteenth was a Tuesday and the twentieth a Wednesday, I had it clearly stated on labels that moved across the top. A visualization of the week.
What are you often looking for in a newspaper heading?[8]

9 In 1986, *Abitare* magazine was going to be twenty-five.
The only thing to do was to paint the masthead silver. It took the whole year to do it.
How do you make an anniversary party last one year without spending any money?

9

You mentioned that sometimes you prefer to do your own photography.

There are photographic ideas that I cannot explain to a photographer, because they are just vague intuitions. And since I do not know how much time it's going to take to find it, I just work alone. When the search is through, I am sometimes in a situation where the only thing left is to press the shutter.

I assume this was the case with the Florence Henri poster and catalogue.

Yes. I knew I wanted to use mirrors. I knew I was going to use
126 her portrait by Lucia Moholy. I knew I wanted her name to be integrated. I wanted integration of the name to make the photograph the poster. I wanted to use that portrait because Lucia Moholy's portraits at the Bauhaus were an appendix to the exhibition. I wanted the mirrors because they were fundamental in Florence Henri's work.
But when I started playing with the mirrors, I had not even a mental sketch. The idea only began to take form when, after fruitless hours, I had the intuition to introduce a second

8. The "Quotidiano" was designed in association with Ray Knobel, Sabina Oberholzer, and Renato Tagli.

portrait that would reflect a reversed face from the back of the first mirror into a second mirror, and from that into a third mirror, reversing the face back to its original state, on a distant plane.

I know you worked a lot with the photographer Serge Libis.

For complex problems, I used to go to Serge. He is so good. Unfortunately, he doesn't want to work anymore. He makes his own wine instead.

98 On the RSt set catalogue, he did the difficult part, the stainless steel objects; I did the easy part, the chicken, the bass, the pretzels with the olives, everything printed in violet.

I remember the constant surprises when I first turned those thirty-two pages in the de Harak office. The chicken, the spaghetti, the eggplant, the fish, suddenly the typographical divertissement of the six logos. An essential journey through type design.
Let's talk about typefaces.
Lou Danziger talked about Gene Federico as being the "Prince of Lightline Gothic." It is difficult to associate you with a specific typeface. The confrontation between past and present occurs often in your choices.

In my posters for the museum, I often use the typeface as a significant cultural witness of the time. The cases of *Les Noces* and of *Lyonel Feininger* are emblematic.

112 Schlemmer worked in 1927 with the director Hermann Scherchen on a project for the setting of the ballet *Les Noces*. It is the last work of the so-called Russian period of Igor Stravinsky. At the Bauhaus since 1920, Schlemmer attempted in this case to develop a specific language, integrating, as Stravinsky had done in his music, remembrances from the Russian popular tradition. In this case, the time span covered by the exhibition was very limited. Stravinsky had worked on *Les Noces* from 1914 to 1923. Schlemmer, as I said, in 1927.

124 In the case of Feininger, who had also been called to the Bauhaus, but in 1919 when he was already forty-eight, the time span covered by the exhibition was much wider, beginning before the turn of the century and continuing until Feininger's death in the fifties. In both cases, Bauhaus typography, in its rich development, could have been a source. But in no way would a puristic or strictly functional typographic approach have been appropriate: in Schlemmer, I had to implement Stravinsky's dissonances; in Feininger, the complexity of his previous artistic itinerary, cubism in particular, and futurism.
In the first case, of the thirty six-letters I needed, twenty-two were "stolen" from Herbert Bayer's alphabets, mostly from the

10 Bauhaus Universal Type variations of 1925. One letter I took from

10
abcdefghi
jklmnopqr
stuvwxyz
a   dᵈ

abcdefghijkl
mnpqrstuvw
xyzag   dᵈ

Theo van Doesburg. Four letters were "assembled," a common practice at the time. The three disks were directly taken from Schlemmer's *The Husband's Prayer*.

In the case of Feininger, the discovery of the ten incredible Itten typographical pages published in *Utopia*, 1921,[9] was decisive for the choice of the main typeface. It is here that I saw Bernhard Roman used in a futurist/functional context, often combined with Fraktur, a typeface that had been used for the captions of Feininger's caricatures. A typeface I knew I was going to use. Other typographical elements were stolen or adapted: the "comb" from the Bauhaus cover of Junge Menschen,[10] and the "rule progression" from the *Farben-Licht-Spiel* cover,[11] a perfect typographical variation on the obsessive progressions Feininger imposed on the wood in his xylographies. The typographical wave border — you know about his passion for water and sailboats — was found in an old typographer's sample book.

To widen the cultural references, I introduced Didot, an homage to his Parisian sojourns, and Stevens Shanks, a sharp, bold sans-serif.

The clash between the big assembled sans-serif F and the Bernhard Roman of the name — a name that I had decomposed three dimensionally according to the laws of cubism — was going to commence the complex typo-cultural journey among the allusive geometric black forms.

This was the only time I used Bernhard Roman.

Do you recollect any other typeface you have used only once?

The first that comes to my mind is Industria. I used it in the *Video Art* poster. The time span of the exhibition was from 1966 to 1996. I wanted a condensed contemporary sans-serif with an obsessive rhythm. I just changed the rounded, and in some ways decadent, capital letter A. I used the V upside down to strengthen the visual connection between "Video" and "Art." I also chopped off the bottom part to strengthen the horizontality of the text arrangement, and juxtaposed and shifted Bodoni Light — Bodoni is the corporate typeface of the museum — to suggest movement and to allude to the deliberate accidents that often occur in art videos.

Details that become fundamental.

"It is like an amazing, well-rehearsed and disciplined circus, all controlled down to the minutest details by ringmaster Bruno Monguzzi… A film sequence in space and time."[12] When F.H.K. Henrion wrote this, he was referring to your Mayakovsky catalogue. You talked about this in the *Eye* interview. Tell me about the Milano Zone series and the use of grids in your book design.

I will try to explain three paradigmatic cases.

9. Johannes Itten had also been called to teach at the Bauhaus in 1919. These pages are reproduced in *Bauhaus typografie*, Dusseldorf: Edition Marzona, 1984, pp. 50-54.
10. Ibid., p. 91.
11. Ibid., p. 88.
12. F.H.K. Henrion, *Top Graphic Design*, Zurich: ABC Verlag, 1983, pp. 102-09.

Majakovskij

Mejerchol'd

Stanislavskij

electa editrice

Mario de Micheli Note sulla poetica di Majakovskij

11

M Z 7

Milano
Zona sette
Bovisa
Dergano

12 In *Milano Zone*, I used a thirty module grid. Five columns, with six modules per column. The column was composed of seventy-seven lines of nine point text. Twelve lines per module, one line in between modules. Since the books mixed essays and interviews, I opposed three horizontal bands to the vertical structure of the written essays to receive the verbal flow of the personal accounts. The very long interviews could run over a double band height. The essays were always set on a single column width, always justified, and always in Bodoni.

The interviews were set flush left-ragged right, and in order to differentiate each person within a given double spread, five different typefaces were introduced in two different weights. The width of the column could also vary from one, to one and one-half, to two columns. Each interview was marked on the top by a rule. The rule would bleed off the page when the interview was continued on the following page. To strengthen continuity, the horizontal bleeding of images was also allowed.

In the second case, the grid is more complex, and the sizes to be used for the images are not based on an elementary system of multiples. The page is structured in accordance with specific functions and dimensional needs.

The Boggeri catalogue fits in this category. For the text section, a simple four column grid was designed, establishing the four margins that were kept in the illustrated section.

13 The catalogue developed from a central row that provided two different heights relating to the A5 and A4 basic formats, stressing horizontal continuity from the 1930s to the 1980s. Complementary mirrored rows could be used at the top and at the bottom of the page.

From the central row, images could be enlarged to reach the top or the bottom line. The full height could also be used. The space separating the juxtaposed images along the rows would increase in accordance with their size.

The captions, set in accordance with the typographical grid of the first section, were all grouped in the upper left corner of the lefthand page, the righthand page whenever the left was used with a full image.

In the third case, functions, dimensions, and positioning belong to an open system where continuity is achieved through other devices, grid constants assuming a marginal role.

The RSt set booklet you had mentioned before is exemplary in this respect.

Typeface and body size are constant, but not the width of the column, nor its positioning. The only other constant — the fundamental one — is the strong, essential treatment of each title: the black underlining bar. It changes length, but is always

13

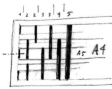

placed at the top, bleeding off to the left on the lefthand pages, to the right on the righthand pages. A true "anaphora" of a visual discourse in continual transformation.

Your uses of photography in solving communications problems are varied. For the poster *Was geht mich der Frühling an…* (*What has Spring got to do with me…*), the solution was derived from imaginative darkroom work.

In 1987, when Heinz Bütler and I worked on the titles and the poster for a documentary he had filmed in a Jewish home for the elderly outside Vienna, he brought a bunch of photographs taken during the shooting. The title of the film, *Was geht mich der Frühling an…* (*What has Spring got to do with me…*), was taken from a conversation between Bütler and one of the residents, Frau Azderbal. I therefore kept only the pictures she was in, and since no close-ups were available, I asked for the negatives. Picked a frame, blew up a small portion, and began to work on the framing of her face. I now had the portrait, but not the poster. What I needed was an image that could tell the story. A picture with the strength of a symbol.
I went back to the darkroom, exposed the strong face, laid a narrow strip of cardboard between two film boxes and exposed again without negative. The diagonal strip of light crossing her face was now telling the story. Words and the colors of spring could follow.

117

You seem to have the courage to appropriately disobey the wrong briefs. A good case in point is the poster competition for the Musée d'Orsay.

In the spring of 1986, a few months before the opening of the new Musée d'Orsay in Paris, a competition to design a poster for the opening was organized, so that a show of the best projects could be held, and the press could talk once more about this impending birth.
There were several hundred entries. Most of them were showing a painting, or a detail from a painting. Others were showing the building, or a detail from the building: the head of Neptune, the great clock, the huge vault. But there were also some avant-gardist designers playing with words, textures, layers, and triangles. The logo was mostly very small, and often pushed in a funny place, probably because to some it looked old fashioned, and to others it would disrupt their compositions.
The head of the curators realized that he did not want to see a painting, not even a detail from a painting; the director did not want to see the building, not even a detail from the building. Both, not knowing anything about graphic design, disregarded

the avant-gardists achievements. So the jury ended up with two second prizes, one third, and no first prize to be printed. Since the poster was to announce the opening, they needed it badly.

Fast. Having designed the logo and the signage, but not having entered the competition for the poster, I was called to Paris.

In a long meeting with Jean Jenger, the director, and Léone Nora, in charge of public relations, we finally realized that the only necessary elements were the logo and the date.

So here I was at home in Meride with a new brief and began to endlessly play around with the date and the logo, the logo and the date, getting nowhere. Nothing was happening, nothing was opening, nothing was beginning. I walked over to my photography books, picked a Lartigue album, and slowly began to go through the pages.

When I came to the image of his brother taking off with a glider that their uncle had constructed at chateau Rouzat, I knew I had the answer. The fly had broken the web.

And here I was, back in Paris again, with Jean Jenger and Léone Nora, knowing I had disobeyed. I was using a photograph, and no image was to be used. Jenger got very upset. He said that we had all agreed that no work of art should appear on the poster. And that anyway it was not "le musée de l'aviation."

I said that it was a metaphor and that the people that knew the logo knew what the museum was all about. I nevertheless added that the poster had to be their poster. That it should belong to them. But Jenger had stopped listening and began to talk to himself pacing nervously up and down the room. I tried to interrupt him, asserting that he did not have to convince me. He said he was thinking. My eyes met the eyes of Madame Nora, which were a bit perplexed, but very beautiful, and we sat down.

Jenger would sometimes stop, look at the poster, and then start his gymnastics all over again. I think he was trying to imagine the possible reactions of all the people he really or virtually knew. A kind of French human comedy with an unexpected end. "Monguzzi," he said, "I am so convinced that the poster is right, that I will bring it myself to Rigaud" (the president of the museum). The following day a worried Madame Nora was on the phone. The Lartigue Foundation does not allow the cropping of Lartigue's photographs. Not knowing which way to turn I asked her to try showing the project to the Foundation anyway. Not only were we allowed to use the photograph as planned, but a vintage print of that shot was given to the museum. It was the fourth Lartigue to enter the collection.

Ten days later, on Friday the 12th of September, at the age of ninety-two, Jacques-Henri Lartigue died. The poster became a posthumous homage. After the museum's opening Florette Lartigue wrote about the project to Jacques Rigaud, expressing how "heureux" her husband had been.

104

I wanted to tell you this story because I assume students
and young designers would read this book. You also have to learn
to have the courage to disobey.
Disobey the wrong briefs; disobey the rules when they don't
allow you to reach the proper goal, disobey fashion, style,
and trends because they limit the range of the possible solutions.
Don't let fashion, style, and trends tear off pages from the
dictionary of visual communication.

Rick Poynor wrote that you have "developed a graphic language
untouched by the passing whims of fashion." What is the relation
of design to the world of fashion (current trends)?[13]

At the beginning of the sixties, in Milan, several Italian designers
asked Grisetti, a small typographer Boggeri used to work with,
to throw away Cairoli or Etrusco, two strong and beautifully
designed sans-serifs, to buy Helvetica. Having no room for another
case, one had to go.
He therefore decided to consult with "the two Swiss" at Boggeri's.
Aldo and I told him that we could do well enough even without
Helvetica. Because Boggeri's lesson was to turn limitations
into advantages, to look for the substance of things — and Grisetti
already had Aksidenz Grotesk. Six point to sixty point in two
weights.
When he left, he seemed perplexed. His Italian designers were
more Swiss than the Swiss. Suddenly it seemed to many that
without Helvetica, no good design could be achieved any more.
What perplexes me is that some of these people, who hated Gill
Sans in the sixties, fell in love with it in the eighties, and found
Helvetica, instead, pretty boring. What were they actually seeing?
What is the relationship between the fundamental characteristic
of a typeface, its weight, its rhythm, how it sets, how it reads,
and the passing whims of fashion?
But fashion is a misleading word. Because the fashion system,
in fashion, never truly affects the nature of the product.
Paradoxically, we could say that nothing really changes. A shoe
remains a shoe, a hat remains a hat.
It's like in automobile design, what you call the body (in fact, it is
the dress) changes every year. But a car remains a car. It doesn't
become a horse or a bicycle.
A bikini or a monokini remains a bathing suit, even in a leopard
print fabric. It does not pretend to become a fur coat.
The fashion designer designs the bikini in different sizes and
various colors.
We could say that he designs, but does not apply, the suit.
The decisive choice is the consumer's choice, putting together
form and content — the bottom with the bottom, the bra
with the breasts.

74 13. Rick Poynor, "Reputations:
Bruno Monguzzi," *Eye* 1, 1990, p. 8.

The graphic designer designs and applies. He inevitably puts a form over a content.

In graphic design, we keep going from bikini to fur coats. Often irrespective of the season. But since we do not catch a cold, we are not even aware.

We keep introducing visual elements repeated massively, but disorganically related to the reference, to the content, to the problem. In the hope of freedom, many graphic designers seem in fact to adapt their "personal" language to visual models that immediately become abused, overused, and then rejected in a kind of contagious visual bulimia.

Every single little hut today has to become a cathedral. When the extraordinary becomes ordinary, something must be wrong.

The fashion system is like a pocket dictionary with continuous revised editions. The only constant in the constant changes is that a lot of words are missing.

I think that changes in design should be dictated by the content, not by the fashion system. New design, as Charles Eames stated, comes from new problems.

To end this conversation, I would like to quote another master, Achille Castiglioni.

"There is not a Castiglioni style. There is a Castiglioni method," he asserted in a recent interview for his MoMA exhibition in New York, a method, he added, of a "designer out of fashion."[14]

14. Gianluigi Nicolin, "Castiglioni: 'Io designer fuori moda.'" *Corriere della Sera*, 20 dicembre 1997, p. 33.

Color Plates

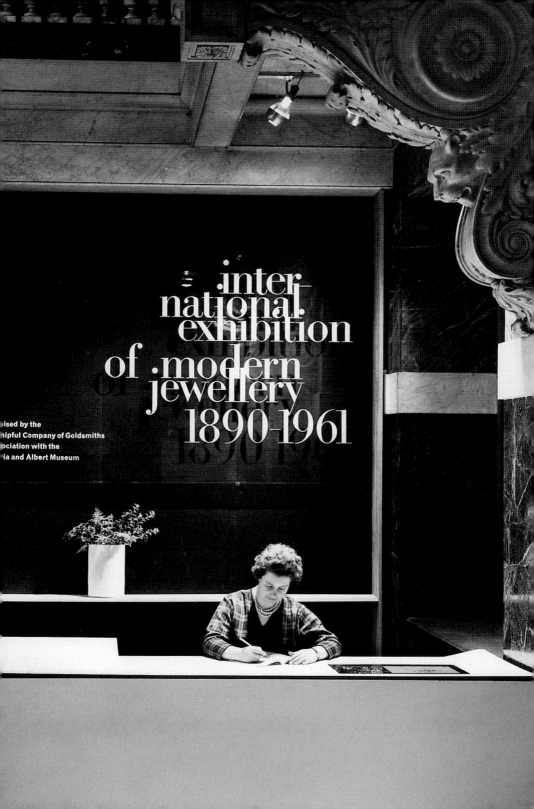

inter-
national
exhibition
of .modern
jewellery
1890-1961

ised by the
hipful Company of Goldsmiths
ociation with the
ia and Albert Museum

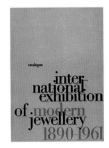

1961
Worshipful Company of Goldsmith,
London
1. *International Exhibition
of Modern Jewellery*
with Dennis Bailey and Alan Irvine
3-7. Catalogues, 21 x 14.8 cm
with Dennis Bailey

1963
City of Liverpool
2. Town Planning Exhibition
with Alan Irvine

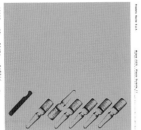

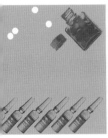

1962
Roche, Milan
8. 9.   Ronicol, Ronicol Compositum
Fold-out brochure
16.3 x 97 cm

1962
Loro e Parisini, Milan
10.   Magutt 205
Advertisement
28 x 21 cm
1961
De Bortoli Arredamenti
11.   Logo

per la bellezza delle vostre mani **guanti satinati** per uso casalingo

1962
Pirelli, Milan
12. Packaging for rubber gloves
10.6 x 33 cm

1962
Pirelli General Electrical Cables,
Milan
13. Study for logo
1969
Pirelli Tires, Milan
14. Logo

Gavina   Marcel Breuer

GAVINA

Bologna San Lazzaro
Italia

Gavina costruit suolonoFour ser fabrica en
Francia avoisi

Marcel Breuer en exclusivité mondiale

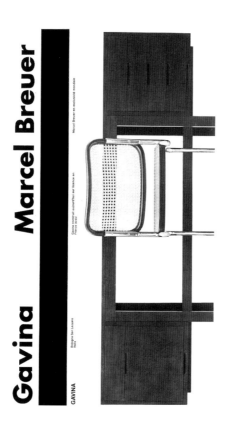

Una piccola sfera...

IBM

Per anni il funzionamento delle macchine per scrivere si è basato sul medesimo principio. Questo era esattamente l'opposto di quanto avviene nella scrittura manuale, dove il foglio è fermo ed è la mano che si sposta da sinistra verso destra. La IBM, ispirandosi appunto alla scrittura manuale, ha realizzato una macchina per scrivere elettrica veramente

rivoluzionaria. Le barre di scrittura od il carrello mobile non sono che un ricordo del passato. Sulla IBM 72 il foglio di carta è fermo, mentre un elemento unico di scrittura a forma sferica e non più grande di una pallina da golf, scorre veloce da sinistra verso destra, imprimendo i caratteri esattamente come la mano che scrive.

Questa piccola sfera può essere sostituita in pochi secondi con un'altra avente caratteri diversi.
Anche la speciale cartuccia del nastro è rapidamente sostituibile.

Una piccola sfera fa della IBM 72 la macchina per scrivere del futuro.

Enea Cerquetti:
Che cos'è la NATO

Jaca Book

Contro
la libertà dei popoli:
l'esercito italiano
come polizia
di uno stato autoritario

Piccola serie 25

Wilfred G Burchett:
Ancora la Corea

Jaca Book

Se il Vietnam rappresenta
una sconfitta del nostro
sistema sociale, questo sistema è egualmente riuscito
ad eclissare in Estremo
Oriente contraddizioni
altrettanto gravi. La prima
è la Corea.

Piccola serie 16

Hosea Jatfe:
Dal colonialismo diretto
al colonialismo indiretto:
il Kenia

Jaca Book

Sull'Africa finora si sono
letti dei «libri».
Rare eccezioni: Malcolm X,
Fanon e pochi altri.
Questo non è un «libro» ma
un semplice e lungo
racconto, una vera lezione
di geografia, storia ed
economia.

Piccola serie 14

Gérard Chaliand:
I contadini
del Nord Vietnam
e la guerra

Jaca Book

in appendice:
Wilfred Burchett
Vietnam: 1945-1968

Piccola serie 28-29

Pierre Jalée:
L'imperialismo
negli anni '70

Jaca Book

Saggi

C Wright Mills:
Sociologia
e pragmatismo

Jaca Book

Saggi xxs

C Wright Mills:
Sociologia e pragmatismo

A cura e con un'introduzione
di Irving Louis Horowitz

Jaca Book

1968
Jaca Book, Milan
19-25. Piccola serie, 20.3 x 12.6 cm
Saggi, Saggi xxs, 23 x 14 cm
1967
Expo '67, Montreal
26. Man the Provider theme pavilion

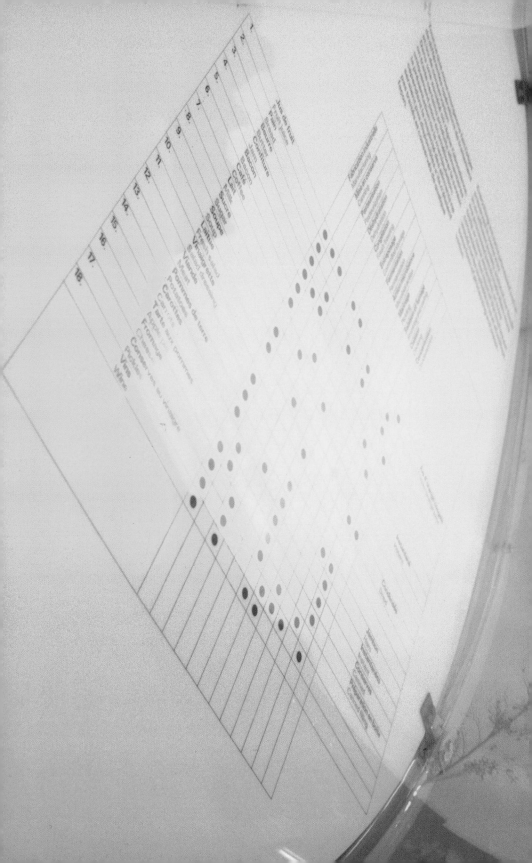

1973
City of Bergamo
27-31. Caravaggio
        Didactic traveling exhibition
28. 29. Assembly schemes
    30. Plan
        with Roberto Sambonet
        and Giancarlo Ortelli

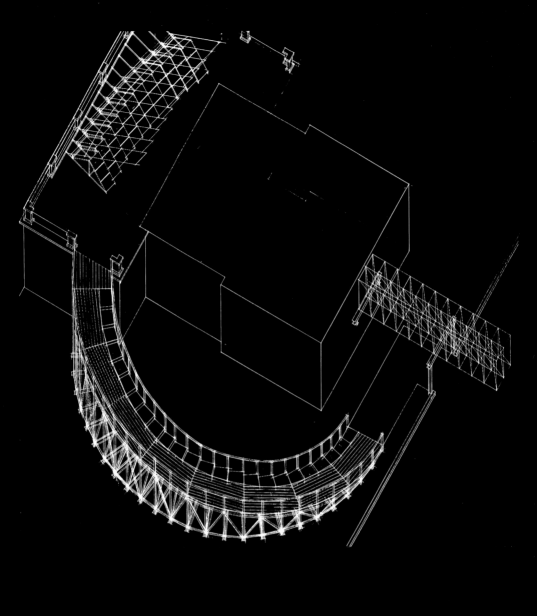

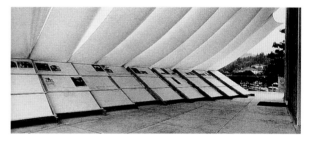

93   1975
            City of Luino
   32-34. *Bernardino Luini*, didactic exhibition
      32. Axonometric drawing of the exterior
            interventions
            with Roberto Sambonet
            and Giancarlo Ortelli

1981
City of Milan
35. For the assistance of earthquake
    victims in Irpinia
    Poster
    98 x 140 cm

1986
Pinacoteca di Brera, Milan
36. Trial for the Brera Museum
    Poster
    138 x 98 cm
    Photo: Guia Sambonet

Processo per il Museo — Brera

Mejerchol'd Stanislavskij Majakovskij

a cura del ministero della cultura dell'urss

comune di milano
ripartizione cultura
regione lombardia
associazione italia-urss

milano
castello sforzesco
sala della balla
dal 2 al 23 aprile 1975 lunedì escluso

ore:
9.30—
12.30
14.30—
17.30

entrata libera

1977
Sambonet SpA, Vercelli
RSt set
42-46. Booklet
22 x 21 cm
Photos: Serge Libis
and Bruno Monguzzi

47. *When?*
Fold-out brochure
66 x 21 cm
Photos: Bruno Monguzzi
48. Packaging
with Roberto Sambonet
and Mario Zachetti

RStset
design: Roberto Sambonet padelle

RStset
design: Roberto Sambonet olio
aceto
sale
pepe

RStset
design: Roberto Sambonet pesciera

RStset
design: Roberto Sambonet coltello pane

RStset
design: Roberto Sambonet servire

RStset
design: Roberto Sambonet forchetta tavola

1.	2.	3.	4.	5.	6.	7.
Pazzia e ritratti ▬▬ disegni di malati e sani di mente 1962-1978	Tavole aritmetiche ▬▬ e scale di colore ripetizione di forme elementari e variazioni di toni primari	Studi organici ▬▬ e disegni esecutivi equilibrio di pesi e alternanza di moti	Strutture modulari ▬▬ e progressioni geometriche, circolarità e profondità degli oggetti	Oggetti di cristallo ▬▬ e oggetti di acciaio secondo le tre componenti materiali pescera, bicchieri empilage, contenitori da forno, vasi ad angolo	Mantova Casa del Mantegna via Acerbi 47 16V-IVI1978 9.30-12.30 15-19 aperto tutti i giorni	Roberto Sambonet Ricerche tra disegno e design

PA ZZ IA

DELLA

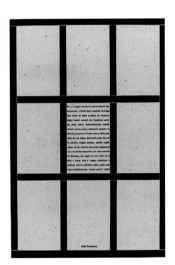

1981
Nidasio Arti Grafiche, Milan
54-58. Promotional brochure
29.7 x 21.5 cm
Photos: Bruno Monguzzi

di parole con cui si vuole indicare indirettamente una persona o una cosa. Ma se nel linguaggio politico (il ritorno cittadino dello stato); o in quello letterario (il bel paese dove il si suona); o in quello giuridico (colui che ho l'onore di difendere) ; la circonlocuzione è spesso un utile artificio...

Circonlocuzione ■ Molto usata nel linguaggio politico, nel linguaggio letterario, nel linguaggio giuridico, è il giro ...nel linguaggio pratico essa appare rischiosa.

"O tu
che con me dividi
la buona
e la cattiva sorte,
vorresti con celerità
d'angelo precipitante
accorciarmi
il bianco discoide
che lento disciogliendosi
lenisce il sussultuoso
terremotare
quando dilacera lassù
dove si forma
immagine e pensiero..."
Meglio dire

Maria,
dammi un'aspirina
che ho mal di testa".

1 per dire il presidente
2 per dire l'Italia
3 per dire il probabile assassino

9 décembre 1986

1986
Musée d'Orsay, Paris
59. Poster for the opening
300 x 400 cm
Photo: Jacques-Henri Lartigue
60-62. Signage
with Gae Aulenti, Roberto Ostinelli,
Gérard Plénacoste, Jean Widmer

Sculpture 1850-1880

86N1098614

Hundert
Franken

Tschient
Francs

Der Präsident
des Bankrates

Ein Mitglied
des Direktoriums

100

Schweizerische Nationalbank
Banca Naziunala Svizra

86N1098614

63.   64-66.

Zehn Franken
Diesch Francs

Schweizerische Nationalbank
Banca Nazionala Svizra

Alberto Giacometti

1901–1966

Mille Francs
Mille Franchi

Banque Nationale Suisse
Banca Nazionale Svizzera

Jacob Burckhardt

1818–1897

Cent Francs
Cento Franchi

Banque Nationale Suisse
Banca Nazionale Svizzera

Le Corbusier

1887–1965

107

1991
Federal Reserve of Switzerland
63-66. Invited competition for a new
banknote series.
The given random pairing
of personality and bill denomination
was changed to create
a chronological sequence.

The series begins
with Alberto Giacometti,
born in 1901
and photographed at the age of 21,
and ends
with Jakob Burckhardt,
born in 1818
and photographed at the age of 74.

1991
Abitare magazine, Milan
67. 68. Covers, 30 x 23.5 cm
Photos: Bruno Monguzzi, Serge Libis
1987
Museo Cantonale d'Arte, Lugano
69. Poster for the opening
128 x 90.5 cm

1987
Museo Cantonale d'Arte, Lugano,
and Kunsthaus, Zurich
70. *The Ticino and its Photographers*
Poster
128 x 271.5 cm
Photos: Roberto Donetta,
Fausto Gerevini

1989
Kunsthaus, Zurich
Photography from the Soviet Union
71. 72. Invitation card
21 x 14.8 cm
73. Poster
128 x 90.5 cm
Photos: S.C. Raoult, Pjotr Orup

Mercoledì			
Giovedì			
Venerdì			
Sabato	10–12	14–18
Martedì			
Domenica		14–18
Lunedì	chiuso	

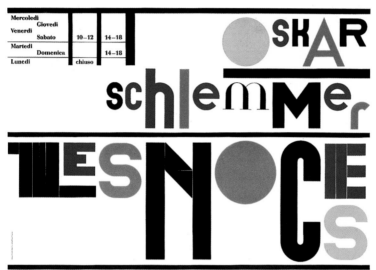

OSKAR schlemMer

LES NOCES

Scenografie, acquerelli, disegni, documenti per la musica di

IGOR STraWINsky

Museo Cantonale d'Arte, Via Canova 10, Lugano   2 Luglio–2 Ottobre 1988

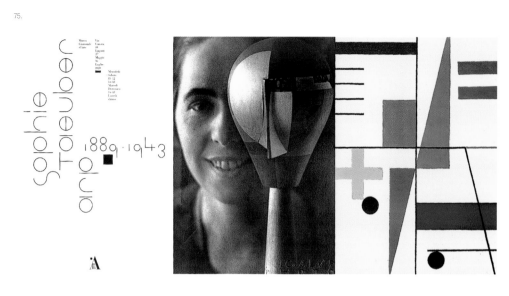

1988
Museo Cantonale d´Arte, Lugano
74. *Les Noces*
Poster, 128 x 90.5 cm
1989
Museo Cantonale d´Arte, Lugano
75. *Sophie Taeuber-Arp*
Poster, 128 x 271.5 cm

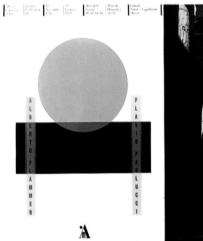

1989
Museo Cantonale d'Arte, Lugano
76. *Alberto Flammer, Flavio Paolucci*
Poster
128 x 271.5 cm
Photos: Alberto Flammer

1991
Dr. Roberto Malacrida, Bellinzona
77-83. Medical Symposiums
Enrollment cards, 10.5 x 21 cm
Fold-out brochures and posters
63 x 21 cm, 63 x 42 cm

115 The fold-out brochures
were made by printing the poster
graphics on both sides of the paper,
then making a vertical cut
right in the middle and folding.

1989
Museo Cantonale d'Arte, Lugano
84. *Pier Francesco Mola*
Masters of the XXth century
from the museum's collection
Poster
128 x 271.5 cm

1988
Al Castello Film Production, Arzo
85. *What has spring*
got to do with me...
Poster
128 x 90.5 cm
Photo: Heinz Butler
and Bruno Monguzzi

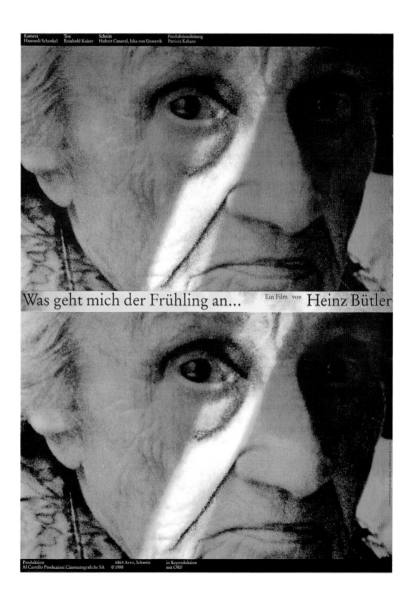

117

Museo Cantonale d'Arte   via Canova 10 Lugano   16 Dicembre 1989–28 Gennaio 1990   Lunedì Natale Capodanno: chiuso

Mercoledì·Sabato 10·12 14·18 Martedì Domenica 14·18

1987 – 1989

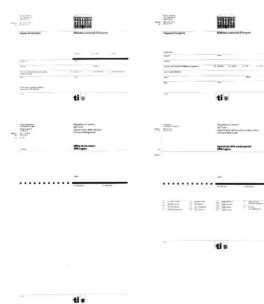

1990
Museo Cantonale d'Arte, Lugano
86. *Nando Snozzi*
   Poster
   128 x 90.5 cm
   1991
87-93. Repubblica e Cantone Ticino
   Examples of corporate identity

1991
Victory Interactive Media, Lugano
94-97. Examples of corporate identity
1987
Al Castello Film Production, Arzo
98-100. Examples of corporate identity

1990
Museo Cantonale d'Arte, Lugano
101. *Fausto Gerevini*
Poster
128 x 90.5 cm
Photo: Bruno Monguzzi

Fausto
Cerevini   1988 /
1990

Museo
Cantonale
d'Arte

Via
Canova
10   Lugano

8
Dicembre
1990
—
27
Gennaio
1991

Fotografie

mercoledì
giovedì
venerdì
sabato   10–12
14–18

martedì   14–18
domenica

lunedì
Natale
Capodanno   chiuso

102.

122

1990
Museo Cantonale d'Arte, Lugano
102. *Fausto Melotti*
      Melotti and Mulas
      Poster
      128 x 271.5 cm
      Photos: Ugo Mulas

1990
Kunsthaus, Zurich
103. *The presence of absence:*
      the photogram in the 20th century
      Poster
      128 x 90.5 cm
      Photogram: Bruno Monguzzi

Anwesenheit
bei Abwesenheit Fotogramme Schweizerische
und die Kunst im Stiftung für
20. Jahrhundert die Photographie

31. März bis 27. Mai 1990

Kunsthaus
Zürich

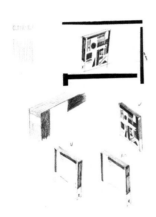

1991
Museo Cantonale d'Arte, Lugano
Lyonel Feininger
104.   Poster, 128 x 90.5 cm
105.   Initial sketches, 21.2 x 16 cm
106-108.   Catalogue, 28 x 25 cm

Florence Henri
Fotografie 1927-1938

Lucia Moholy
Ritratti al Bauhaus

Mercoledì–Domenica 10–17 Martedì 11–17
Lunedì: 24, 25, 26, 31 dicembre e Capodanno chiuso

7 dicembre '91–26 gennaio '92

Museo Cantonale d'Arte   Via Canova 10   Lugano

1991
        Museo Cantonale d'Arte, Lugano
        Florence Henri, Lucia Moholy
    109. Poster, 128 x 90.5 cm
110-112. Invitation cards, 10.5 x 21 cm
    113. Catalogue, front and back cover
        28 x 23 cm
        Photo: Bruno Monguzzi

1991
Museo Cantonale d'Arte, Lugano
Florence Henri
114-125. Catalogue
28 x 23 cm

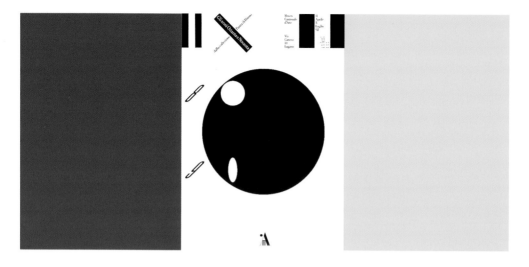

126.

1992
Museo Cantonale d'Arte, Lugano
126. *The Eighties and the Nineties
in the Panza di Biumo Collection*
Poster, 128 x 271.5 cm
127. *Luciano Rigolini, Adriana Beretta*
Poster, 128 x 90.5 cm
Photos: Bruno Monguzzi

adriana beretta
adriana beretta
adriana beretta
adriana beretta

fotografie '90—'92

12.12.
1992
14.02.
1993

Museo Cantonale d'Arte
Lugano
via
Canova 10

'90—'92
installazioni e tele

luciano

angelini

adriana beretta
adriana beretta
adriana beretta
adriana beretta

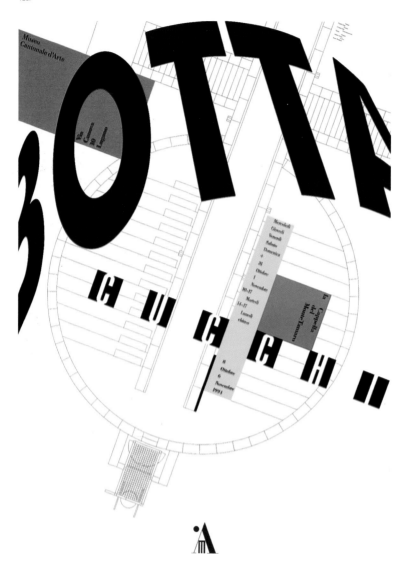

1994
Museo Cantonale d'Arte, Lugano
128. *Botta/Cucchi:*
The Monte Tamaro Chapel
Poster
128 x 90.5 cm

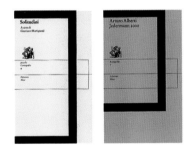

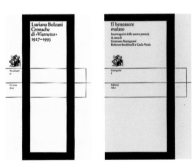

133

1987
Alice Edizioni, Lugano
129-130. Piccole cartografie, Autografie
20.5 x 12.5 cm
131-134. Arcipelaghi, Cartografie, Sconfini,
Corbaro
23 x 14 cm

1996
Museo Cantonale d'Arte, Lugano
135-137. Sguardi sulla collezione series
21 x 15 cm

da
Dürer
a
Klee

**Museo
Cantonale
d'Arte**

Via Canova
10
Lugano

la
**Rappresentazione
dell'Ignoto**

Disegni
e
incisioni

**Roberto
Donetta**

pioniere
della
fotografia
nel
Ticino
di inizio
secolo

24
Aprile
6
Giugno
1993

Martedì
14–17
Mercoledì Domenica
10–17
Lunedì chius.

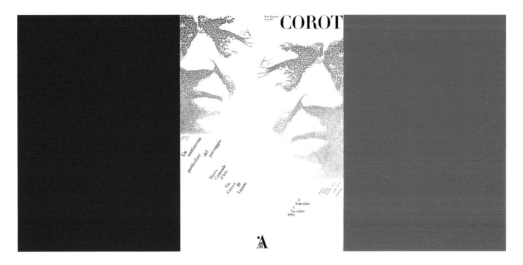

1995
Museo Cantonale d'Arte, Lugano
140. *Kandinsky in the Swiss collections*
Poster
128 x 271.5 cm

1994
Museo Cantonale d'Arte, Lugano
Galleria Gottardo, Lugano
Museo del Malcantone, Curio
141. *Ticino and St. Petersburg*
Poster
128 x 90.5 cm
with Alberto Bianda

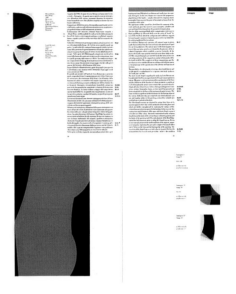

139   1995
Museo Cantonale d'Arte, Lugano
Livio Bernasconi
Hans Knuchel
142.   Poster, 128 x 90.5 cm
143, 144.   Invitation cards, 10.5 x 21 cm
145-147.   Catalogue, 24 x 22 cm

1996
Museo Cantonale d'Arte, Lugano
Video Art '66-'96
148. Folder cover, 24 x 22 cm
149.150. Invitation cards, 10.5 x 21 cm
151. Poster, 128 x 90.5 cm

1996
School of Architecture
Virginia Tech, Blacksburg
152. Ferrari Symposium
Poster, 80 x 54 cm
Photo: Bruno Monguzzi

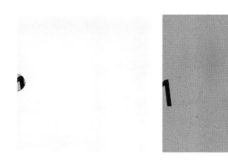

1997
Museo Cantonale d'Arte, Lugano
Fragile
153. Poster, 128 x 90.5 cm
154.155. Invitation cards, 10.5 x 21 cm
156.157. Order forms, 21 x 10.5 cm
158.159. Catalogue,
Box and Cover, 24 x 22 cm

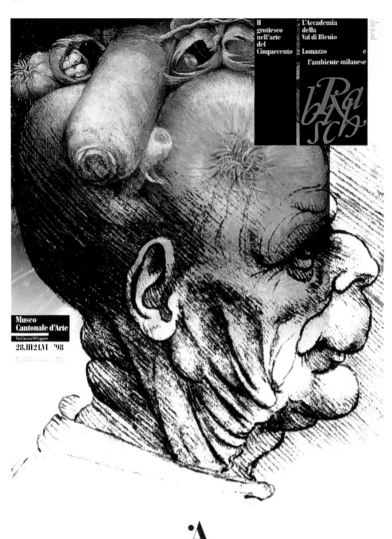

1998
Museo Cantonale d'Arte, Lugano
160. *Rabisch: the grotesque
in the art of the 16th century*
Poster
128 x 90.5 cm

Appendix

1941	Born 21 August, Mendrisio, Switzerland.
	Childhood and schooling in Chiasso, located on the Swiss/Italian border.
1956	Family moves to Geneva.
	Enters École des Arts Décoratifs in Geneva to study Graphic Design.
1960	Moves to London to study typography, photography, and Gestalt Psychology at St. Martin's School of Art & Crafts, Central School of Design, and London School of Printing.
1961—1963	Meets Antonio Boggeri and begins work with Studio Boggeri in Milan.
1963—1965	Invited to be lecturer of Gestalt and Typography at the Cini Foundation in Venice.
	Writes book on typography, *Note per una tipografia informativa,* published by the Cini Foundation.
1965—1967	The office of Charles Gagnon and James Volkus invites Monguzzi to Montreal to design nine pavilions for the Expo '67 World Exhibition.
1967	Designs logo for the comprehensive program of the Metropolitan Transportation Authority of New York (Metra).
	Designs corporate identity proposal for the Canadian National Film Board, for which the new name Canadian Communication Center (CCC) was proposed.
	Both Metra and Film Board projects were never realized.
1968	Returns to Milan.
	Sets the typographical standards for Jaca Book, a small new publishing house.
	Reestablishes contact with Antonio Boggeri and collaborates on an independent basis until the closing of Studio Boggeri in 1981.
1969	Marries Anna Boggeri and buys a house in Meride, a secluded village in the hills of southern Switzerland.
1970	Son Nicolas is born.
	Joins faculty at Lugano School of Design to teach the Psychology of Perception and Typographic Design, where he continues today.
1971	Receives Bodoni Prize for contributing to the improvement of typographic design in Italy.
	Designs corporate identity for Sambonet SpA, Vercelli, Italy.
	Begins collaboration with Roberto Sambonet and Giancarlo Ortelli on exhibition design projects.
1972	Designs *Raffaello, lo Sposalizio della Vergine*, an exhibition at the Pinacoteca di Brera in Milan.
1973	Designs *Immagine del Caravaggio*, a didactic travelling exhibition originating at the Palazzo della Ragione in Bergamo, Italy.
1974	Daughter Elisa is born.
	His work with Roberto Sambonet is exhibited at Museo de Arte in São Paolo.
1975	Designs *Bernardino Luini* exhibition in Luino and *Majakovskij Mejerchol'd Stanislavskij* exhibition at the Castello Sforzesco in Milan.
1976	Designs *Processo per il Museo–Brera* exhibition at the Pinacoteca di Brera in Milan.
	His work with Roberto Sambonet is exhibited at Artek in Helsinki, Finland.
1977	Designs *Della Pazzia* portfolio, which is exhibited at M'Arte Gallery in Milan.
	Milan Art Directors Club honors Monguzzi, Roberto Sambonet, and Mario Zacchetti with Packaging Design Award for RSt set, a comprehensive packaging program for cutlery, cookware, flatware, and tableware.
1978	*Della Pazzia* portfolio is exhibited at the Casa del Mantegna in Mantova, Italy.
1979	Designs the Italsider Pavilion at the Milan Fair.
	Becomes member of the Alliance Graphique Internationale (AGI).

Writes and designs *Leonardo,* a children's book, with son Nicolas and daughter Elisa. His work with Roberto Sambonet is exhibited at Palazzo Bagatti Valsecchi in Milan.	1980
Edits and designs catalogue *Lo Studio Boggeri, 1933-1981*; curates and designs exhibition of the same title at the Milan Triennale. IBM Fellow at Aspen Design Conference, Colorado.	1981
Lectures at Cooper Union School for the Advancement of Arts and Science in New York; Alfred University, Alfred, NY; AGI/Icograda Student Seminar in Paris; and Kent State University Summer Workshop in Florence, Italy.	1982
Writes and designs "Piet Zwart: L'opera tipografica/The Typographical Work, 1923-1933," a special issue of *Rassegna* magazine on the Dutch design pioneer.	1982—1986
Wins international competition for the visual identity and signage for the new Musée d'Orsay, and works in association with the Paris office of Visuel Design Jean Widmer, and the architect Gae Aulenti until the opening of the museum in 1986. Lectures at the Kent State University Summer Workshop in Florence, Italy.	1983
Lectures at the Kent State University Summer Workshop in Rapperswil, Switzerland.	1985
Art Consultant to the architecture and interior design magazine *Abitare,* published in Milan.	1986—1991
Designs logo for Museo Cantonale d'Arte and, as sole designer, has designed all visual communications materials published by the museum through the present. Speaker at the AGI Congress at Bürgenstock, Switzerland. Lectures at Kent State University to University and College Designers Association Summer Course; Cooper Union School for the Advancement of Arts and Science, New York; American Institute of Graphic Arts, New York; North Carolina State University, Raleigh; Kansas State University, Kansas City. Begins book design collaboration with Associazione Alice, a nonprofit organization whose main scope is to address drug addiction. The books are awarded The Most Beautiful Swiss Books prize in 1996.	1987
Lectures at AGI/Icograda Student Seminar, London; Rochester Institute of Technology, Rochester, NY; and Alfred University, Alfred, NY. Awarded The Best Swiss Posters of the Year prize thirteen times through 1997.	1988
Declines offer to become Director of Graduate Studies in Graphic Design at Yale University School of Art.	1989
One of twelve Swiss designers invited by the Swiss National Bank to design new currency for the Federation. Honored by New York Art Directors Club with Gold Medal Award.	1990
Awarded the Janus Prize by the French government for the work done for Musée d'Orsay. Awarded silver and bronze medals at the Toyama Poster Triennial. Appointed Design Consultant to the Ticino State Government; his work in the field of educational publishing is awarded The Most Beautiful Swiss Books prize in 1997.	1991
Solo exhibition at the Maison du livre, de l'image et du son, Villeurbanne, Lyon, France. Lectures at Portland School of Art Summer Course, Portland, ME, and at Virginia Tech, Blacksburg, VA.	1992
Solo exhibition at Migros-Hochaus, Zurich.	1993
Honored by "10 vor 10" cultural television program and *Hochparterre* architectural design magazine in Zürich with Best Swiss Typographer of the Year award.	1994

1995	Juror at the Festival de l'Affiche, Chaumont, France. Juror of the Logo and Signage Competition for the Bibliothèque Nationale de France, Paris. Speaker at the Icograda Congress in Lisbon.
1996	Juror of the Logo Design Competition for the National Swiss Exhibition 2001. Assumes position as Visiting Professor at Mendrisio Academy of Architecture. Presented with special award from German Open, German Prize for Communication, Essen.
1997	The Museo Cantonale d'Arte celebrates its tenth anniversary by exhibiting all visual communications work designed by Monguzzi for the museum. Juror at the Toyama Poster Triennial, Toyama, Japan. Lectures at the Japan Graphic Designers Association in Tokyo. Presented with the Tokyo Type Directors Club Award and special award from German Open, German Prize for Communication, Essen.
1998	Speaker at the AGI Congress in Toronto. The exhibition *Bruno Monguzzi: A Designer's Perspective* opens at the University of Maryland, Baltimore County. Lectures to the University of Maryland, Baltimore County, and the Baltimore Chapter of the American Institute of Graphic Arts.
1999—2000	The exhibition *Bruno Monguzzi: A Designer's Perspective* begins its national tour.
2000	Solo exhibition at GGG Gallery in Tokyo and DDD Gallery in Osaka.

Selected Publications
on Bruno Monguzzi

Books

Amstutz, Walter, ed.
Who's Who 2.
    Dübendorf: De Clivo Press,
    1982.
Blackwell, Lewis.
Twentieth Century Type.
    London: Calman & King
    Publishing,
    1992.
Cato, Ken, ed.
First Choice 1.
    Tokyo: Graphic-Sha
    Publishing Co.,
    1989.
Cato, Ken, ed.
First Choice 2.
    Roseville East Australia:
    Craftsman House,
    1996.
de Harak, Rudolph, ed.
Posters by Members of the Alliance
Graphique Internationale 1960-1985.
    New York: Rizzoli,
    1986.
Due Dimensioni.
    Milan: Nava,
    1964.
Fisher, Max.
50 Years: Swiss Posters Selected
by the Federal Department of Home
Affairs, 1941-1990.
    Geneva: APG SGA,
    1991.
Fossati, Paolo, and Roberto
Sambonet.
Lo Studio Boggeri 1933-1973:
Comunicazione Visuale e Grafica
Applicata.
    Milan: Pizzi Editore,
    1974.
Friedl, Friedrich, Nicolaus Ott, and
Bernard Stein.
Typography: An Encyclopedic Survey
of Type Design and Techniques
Throughout History.
    New York: Black Dog &
    Leventhal Publishers,
    1998.
Friedl, Friedrich, Nicolaus Ott, and
Bernard Stein.
When, Who, How
Typography.
    Köln: Könemann,
    1998.
Fronzoni, A.G.
Marchio Progetti, Proposte per
il Credito Industriale Sardo.
    Milan: Triennale di Milano,
    1989.
Gottschall, Edward M.
Typographic Communications Today.
    Cambridge: MIT Press,
    1989.
Grieshaber, Judith M.,
and Manfred Kröplien.
Graphic Design: The Raw and the
Cooked.
    Stuttgart: Edition Cantz,
    1989.

Halbey, Hans Adolf,
and Wilhelm Kumm.
Scriptura '93: Schrift Im Plakat.
    Darmstadt: Echo Verlag,
    1992.
Henrion, F.H.K.
AGI Annals.
    Tokyo: Graphic Sha,
    1989.
Henrion, F.H.K.
Top Graphic Design.
    Zurich: Abc Verlag,
    1983.
Herdeg, Walter, ed.
Graphis Annual.
    Zurich: Graphis Press,
    1978, 1979.
Herdeg, Walter, ed.
Photographis
    Zurich: Graphis Press,
    1972.
Hochuli, Jost.
Book Design In Switzerland.
    Zurich: Pro Helvetia,
    1993.
Hochuli, Jost, and Robin Kinross.
Designing Books: Practice and
Theory.
    London: Hyphen Press,
    1996.
Hohenegger, Alfred.
Form and Sign.
    Rome: Romana Libri Alfabeto,
    1977.
Igarashi, Takenobu.
Letterheads, A Collection From
Around The World.
    Tokyo: Graphic Sha,
    1986.
Igarashi, Takenobu.
World Trademarks and Logotypes II.
    Tokyo: Graphic Sha,
    1987.
Iiyama, Genji.
International Corporate Identity 1990.
    Tokyo: Robundo,
    1990.
Jubert, Roxane.
La Typographie Moderne, Postérité
des Avant-Gardes.
    Paris: Mémoire de fin d'étude,
    Ecole Nationale Supérieure
    des Arts Décoratifs,
    1994.
Julier, Guy.
20th Century Design and Designers.
    London: Thames and Hudson,
    1993.
Kamekura, Yusaku, Milton Glaser,
Alain Weill, and Steven Heller, eds.
The 100 Best Posters from Europe and
the United States 1945-1990.
    Tokyo: Toppan Printing Co.,
    1995.
Livingston, Alan and Isabella.
Graphic Design and Designers.
    London: Thames and Hudson,
    1992.

Locher, Adalbert.
Made In Switzerland.
Les Arts Appliqués au Tessin,
    Zurich: Editions
    Hochparterre,
    1977.
Milani, Armando, ed.
A Double Life of 80 AGI Designers.
    San Mauro Torinese: Burgo,
    1996.
Morgan, Ann Lee, ed.
Contemporary Designers.
    London: Macmillan
    Publishers,
    1984.
Müller-Brockmann, Josef,
and Karl Wobmann.
*Photo Plakate: Von den Anfangen
bis zur Gegenwaut.*
    Stuttgart: AT Verlag Aarau,
    1989.
Nagai, Kazumasa,
and Mooto Nakamishi.
*World Graphic Design Now, 4,
Corporate Identity.*
    Tokyo: Kodamasha,
    1989.
Naylor, Colin, ed.
Contemporary Designers 2.
    Chicago: St. James Press,
    1990
Nunoo-Quarcoo, Franc,
and Cynthia M. Wayne.
*Word+Image: Swiss Poster Design
1955-1997.*
    Baltimore: Albin O. Kuhn
    Library Gallery,
    University of Maryland,
    Baltimore County,
    1998.
Odermatt, Siegfrid.
100+3 Swiss Posters.
    Zurich: Waser Verlag,
    1998.
Pedersen, B. Martin, ed.
Graphis Posters 91.
    Zurich: Graphis Press,
    1991.
Pedersen, B. Martin, ed.
Best of Graphis Typography.
    Singapore: Page One
    Publishing,
    1993.
Pedersen, B. Martin, ed.
Graphis Typography 1.
    Zurich: Graphis Press,
    1994.
Pubblicità in Italia.
    Milan: Editrice l'ufficio
    Moderno,
    1963; 1964; 1971-1981.
Rotzler, Willy, Fritz Scharer,
and Karl Wobmann.
Das Plakat in der Schweiz.
    Zurich: Edition Stemmle,
    1990.
Rüegg, Ruedi.
*Basic Typography: Design
with Letters.*
    Zurich: Abc Verlag,
    1989.

*Top Symbols and Trademarks
of the World.*
    Milan: Deco Press,
    1973.
Vigue, Jordi, Norberto Calabro,
and John Clark.
Diseno Tipografico.
    Barcelona: Parramon
    Ediciones, S.A.,
    1993.
Waibl, Heinz.
*Alle Radici della Comunicazione
Visiva Italiana.*
    Como: Centro cultura
    grafica,
    1988.
Who's Who In Graphic Design.
    Zurich: Werd Verlag,
    1994.

Exhibition Catalogues

Anceschi, Giovanni.
*L'Italie Aujourd'hui | L'Italia Oggi
Aspetti della Creatività Italiana
dal 1970 al 1985.*
    Firenze: La casa Usher,
    1985.
Andreas, Jonas-Edel.
Kunst im Anschlag.
    Köln: Museums
    für Angewandte Kunst Köln,
    1996.
Art & Pub, Art e Publicité 1890-1990.
    Paris: Centre Georges
    Pompidou,
    1990.
Bio 11.
    Biennial of Industrial Design.
    Ljubljana: Yugoslavia,
    1986.
Festa de la Lletra.
    Barcelona: Ajuntament
    de Barcelona,
    1979.
*The 5th International Poster Triennial
in Toyama 1997.*
    Toyama: The Museum
    of Modern Art, Japan,
    1997.
Helsinki Poster Biennial '95.
    XI International Poster
    Biennial in Finland.
    Helsinki,
    1995.
Helsinki Poster Biennial '97.
    XII International Poster
    Biennial in Finland.
    Helsinki,
    1997.
*International Poster Triennial
in Toyama, 1985-1994.*
    Toyama: The Museum
    of Modern Art, Japan,
    1996.
The Most Beautiful Swiss Books.
    Bern: Department des Innern,
    Bundesamt für Kultur,
    1996; 1997.
*Ogaki International Invitational
Poster Exhibition.*
    Ogaki: Ogaki Poster Museum,
    1996.
Symbol Logo AGI.
*Trademarks and Symbols
by AGI Members.*
    Brno, Czechoslovakia:
    AGI,
    1989.
*Tenth Colorado Invitational Poster
Exhibition.*
    Fort Collins: Colorado State
    University,
    1997.
*The 3rd International Poster Triennial
in Toyama.*
    Toyama: The Museum
    of Modern Art, Japan,
    1991.

12 Grafici dell'AGI.
  Milan: AGI, Olivetti,
  1984.
Visual Design:
50 Anni di Produzione Italiana.
  Milan: Idealibri,
  1984.
Weill, Alain, ed.
Exposons Affichons...
  Cinquièmes Rencontres
  Internationales des Arts
  Graphiques.
  Ville de Chaumont, France,
  1994.
Weill, Alain, ed.
Jeux de Lettres.
  Huitièmes Rencontres
  Internationales des Arts
  Graphiques.
  Ville de Chaumont, France,
  1997.

Magazine Articles

Besemer, Hans Christian.
"Bruno Monguzzi."
  Novum Gebrauchsgraphik 9,
  1983.
Boggeri, Antonio.
"Bruno Monguzzi."
  Graphis, 209,
  1980.
Campana, Mara.
"È Design."
  Linea Grafica, 1/86,
  1986.
Campana, Mara.
"La trama sorprendente,
Progetti di Bruno Monguzzi."
  Linea Grafica, 6,
  1989.
Campana, Mara.
"Un'immagine lunga 10 anni,
Bruno Monguzzi per il Museo
Cantonale d'Arte di Lugano."
  Linea Grafica, 1/98,
  1998.
Cerri, Pierluigi.
"Il Campo della Grafica Italiana,"
"Il disegno di un libro,"
"L'espressione e il contenuto,"
"Processo per il museo."
  Rassegna 6,
  1981.
Colonetti, Aldo.
"Forma e Contenuto."
  Linea Grafica, 5/90,
  1990.
Federico, Gene.
"Bruno Monguzzi."
  Creation, 13,
  1992.
Federico, Gene.
"Bruno Monguzzi."
  IDEA, 267,
  1998.
Finck, Heinz Deeter.
"Schweizer National Bank
Banknoten."
  Werbung Publicitè, 4.90,
  1990.
Gantenbein, Köbi.
"Spiele mit Lesen und Sehen."
  Hochparterre, 12/94,
  1994.
"German Open: German Prize for
Communication Design."
  Form, 151/3,
  1995.
Gottschalk, Fritz.
"'Swiss Design' Armin Hofmann,
Bruno Monguzzi, Odermatt & Tissi,
Ruedi Kulling, Werner Jeker."
  *The New Edition of Design
  Exchange 12,*
  1997.
"100 Graphic Designers
of the World."
  IDEA, 240,
  1993.

Henrion, F.H.K.
"Type, Pure Type and Type Alone."
  Design and Art Direction,
  1983.
Hochuli, Jost.
"Book Design In Switzerland."
  *Baseline International
  Typographics Journal 22,*
  1996.
Miranda, Oswaldo, ed.
"Bruno Monguzzi."
  *Grafica Magazine
  International,* 40,
  1993.
Müller, Rolf.
"Bruno Monguzzi."
  High Quality, 4,
  1986.
Poyner, Rick.
"Reputations: Bruno Monguzzi."
  Eye, 1,
  1990.
Szeemann, Harald.
"Creativity in Switzerland in the
Fields of Science, Philosophy,
Technology and Art."
  Swissair Gazette, 11,
  1994.
"Typography – [Ad Infinitum]."
  IDEA, Special Issue 256,
  1996.
Wicki, Stephan.
"'Aushängeschild der Schweizer
Grafik.' Werner Jeker, Bruno
Monguzzi, Niklaus Troxler."
  Basler Magazin, 12, Basel,
  1991.
Wlassikoff, Michel.
"Bruno Monguzzi:
Exposition à la Maison du Livre
de l'image et du son, Villeurbanne."
  Signes, 7,
  1992.

Publications
by Bruno Monguzzi

Books

Lo Studio Boggeri,
1933-1981.
Milan: Electa Editrice,
1981.
Note per una tipografia informativa.
Venice: Fondazione Cini,
1964.
Piet Zwart: L'opera tipografica/
The Typographical Work,
1923-1933.
Bologna: Rassegna 30,
1987.

Catalogue

Bruno Monguzzi.
Design à la Maison du livre
de l'image et du son.
Villeurbanne, Lyon,
1992.

Articles

"Appunti sul menabò del libro per
bambini Leonardo."
Il progetto grafico:
venti interventi nel nostro
quotidiano.
Società Unimantaria,
1982.
"Autobiographical Note."
IDEA, 267,
1998.
"La mosca e la ragnatela, ovverossia
l'Italia e la Svizzera."
Grafici Italiani,
edited by Giorgio Camuffo.
Venezia: Canal & Stamperia,
1997.
"Piet Zwart."
Graphis, 258,
1988.
"Piet Zwart:
The Typographical Work 1923-33."
Essays on Design 1
AGI's Designers of Influence.
London: Booth-Clibborn
Editions,
1997.
"Svizzera: l'immagine
della comunicazione urbana."
Abitare, 206,
1982.

Roberto Sambonet
Museu de Arte, São Paolo,
1974.
Roberto Sambonet
Artek, Helsinki,
1976.
Della Pazzia
Galleria M'Arte, Milan,
1977.
Della Pazzia
Casa del Mantegna, Mantova,
1978.
Festa de la Lletra
Galeries Ciento, Eude, Joan
Prats, Sala Gaspar i BCD
Barcelona, Spain,
1979.
Roberto Sambonet
Palazzo Bagatti Valsecchi,
Milan,
1980.
Il Progetto Grafico
Venti interventi
nel nostro quotidiano,
Società Umanitaria
Travelling Exhibition
Milano,
1981.
Lo Studio Boggeri 1933-1981
Triennale di Milano, Milan,
1981.
Della Pazzia
Public Library, Pound Ridge,
New York,
1982.
Visual Design:
50 anni di produzione in Italia
Arengario, Milan,
1983.
L'Image des mots
Centre Georges Pompidou,
Paris,
1985.
L'Italie Aujourd'hui/L'Italia Oggi
Centre National
d'Art Contemporain
Villa Arson, Nice, France,
1985.
Bio 11
Biennial of Industrial Design
Ljublijana, Yugoslavia,
1986.
AGI Italie
Ancien Manège, Chambéry,
France,
1986.
L'Image de la lettre
Centre Georges Pompidou,
Paris,
1987.
International Exhibition of Graphic
Design and Visual Communications
Zagreb, Yugoslavia,
1987.
Best Swiss Posters of the Year 1987
Travelling Exhibition,
1988.
Graphic Design Biennial
Brno, Czechoslovakia,
1988.

Images d'utilité publique
Centre Georges Pompidou,
Paris,
1988.
Best Swiss Posters of the Year 1988
Travelling Exhibition,
1989.
Marchio Progetti
Proposte per il Credito Industriale
Sardo
Triennale di Milano
Milan,
1989.
Projects for the New Swiss Bank
Notes
Swiss National Bank, Bern,
1989.
Symbol Logo AGI
Trademarks and Symbols
by AGI Members
Brno, Czechoslovakia,
1989.
Best Swiss Posters of the Year 1989
Travelling Exhibition,
1990.
Mexico Poster Biennial
Mexico City,
1990.
Swiss Posters
The New Mornington
Peninsula Arts Centre,
Mornington, Australia,
1990.
Best Swiss Posters of the Year 1990
Travelling Exhibition,
1991.
Deuxièmes rencontres internatio-
nales des arts graphiques
Chaumont, France,
1991.
Mehr Werte
Schweiz und Design: die 80er
Museum für Gestaltung,
Zurich,
1991.
The 3rd International Poster
Triennial in Toyama
The Museum of Modern Art
Toyama, Japan,
1991.
Bruno Monguzzi
Maison du livre, de l'image
et du son
Villeurbanne, Lyon, France,
1992.
Graphic Design Biennial
Brno, Czechoslovakia,
1992.
Mexico Poster Biennial
Mexico City,
1992.
Book Design in Switzerland
Travelling Exhibition
St. Gallen, Switzerland,
1993.
Ogaki International Invitational
Poster Exhibition
Ogaki Poster Museum, Ogaki,
Japan,
1993.

Plakate von Bruno Monguzzi
　　Migros-Hochhaus, Zurich,
　　1993.
Exposons Affichons...
　　Cinquièmes rencontres
　　internationales des arts
　　graphiques
　　Chaumont, France,
　　1994.
Mexico Poster Biennial
　　Mexico City,
　　1994.
Best Swiss Posters of the Year 1994
　　Travelling Exhibition,
　　1995.
German Prize
for Communication Design
　　Design Zentrum, Essen,
　　Germany 1995.
Helsinki Poster Biennial '95
　　XI International
　　Poster Biennial in Finland
　　Helsinki,
　　1995.
The 100 Best Posters from Europe
and the United States 1945-1990
　　International Touring
　　Exhibition, Tokyo,
　　1995.
Best Swiss Posters of the Year 1995
　　Travelling Exhibition,
　　1996.
Kunst Im Anschlag
　　Museums für Angewandte
　　Kunst, Cologne, Germany,
　　1996.
Ogaki International Invitational
Poster Exhibition
　　Ogaki Poster Museum, Ogaki,
　　Japan,
　　1996.
Mexico Poster Biennial
　　Mexico City,
　　1996.
Typo Plakate
　　Rathaus, Willisau,
　　Switzerland,
　　1996.
Best Swiss Posters of the Year 1996
　　Travelling Exhibition,
　　1997.
Bruno Monguzzi.
L'immagine grafica del Museo
Cantonale d'Arte
　　Museo Cantonale d'Arte,
　　Lugano, Switzerland,
　　1997.
The Tenth Colorado International
Invitational Poster Exhibition
　　Fort Collins, Colorado,
　　1997.
The 5th International Poster Triennial
in Toyama
　　The Museum of Modern Art
　　Toyama, Japan,
　　1997.
German Prize
for Communication Design
　　Design Zentrum, Essen,
　　Germany,
　　1997.

Helsinki Poster Biennial '97
　　XII International
　　Poster Biennial in Finland
　　Helsinki,
　　1997.
Jeux de Lettres
　　Huitièmes rencontres
　　internationales des arts
　　graphiques
　　Chaumont, France,
　　1997.
Word+Image:
Swiss Poster Design,
1955-1997
　　Albin O. Kuhn Library
　　& Gallery
　　University of Maryland,
　　Baltimore County
　　Baltimore, Maryland,
　　1998.
Best Swiss Posters of the Year 1997
　　Travelling Exhibition,
　　1998.
Film Plakate
　　Rathaus, Willisau,
　　Switzerland,
　　1998.
German Prize
for Communication Design
　　Design Zentrum, Essen,
　　Germany 1998.
Bruno Monguzzi:
A Designer's Perspective
　　Fine Arts Gallery
　　University of Maryland,
　　Baltimore County
　　Baltimore, Maryland,
　　1998.

Selected
Collections

Centre Georges Pompidou
	Paris
Deutsches Plakat Museum
	Essen
Kunstgewerbemuseum
	Zurich
Maison du livre et de l'affiche
	Chaumont, France
Musée de l'Affiche
	Paris
Museum of Modern Art
	New York
Museum of Modern Art
	Toyama
Museums für Angewandte Kunst
	Cologne
Ogaki Poster Museum
	Ogaki
Poster Museum
	Fort Collins, Colorado
Stedelijk Museum
	Amsterdam

Ades, Dawn.
*The 20th Century Poster: Design
of the Avant-Garde.*
New York: Abbeville Press,
1984.
Alexander, Christopher.
Notes on the Synthesis of Form.
Cambridge: Harvard
University Press,
1964.
Apostolos-Cappadona, Diane, and
Bruce Altshuler. *Isamu Noguchi:
Essays and Conversations.*
New York: Harry N. Abrams
Publishers,
1994.
Arnheim, Rudolf.
Art and Visual Perception.
Berkeley: University
of California Press,
1954.
Arnheim, Rudolf.
*Entropy and Art: An Essay on
Disorder and Order.*
Berkeley, Los Angeles,
and London: University
of California Press,
1971.
Arnheim, Rudolf.
Film as Art.
Berkeley: University
of California Press,
1957.
Arnheim, Rudolf.
New Essays on the Psychology of Art.
Berkeley: University
of California Press,
1986.
Arnheim, Rudolf.
Visual Thinking.
Berkeley: University
of California Press,
1980.
Aynsley, Jeremy.
*Nationalism and Internationalism:
Design in the 20th Century.*
London: Victoria & Albert
Museum,
1993.
Baljeu, Joost.
Theo Van Doesburg.
New York: McMillan
Publishers,
1974.
Bayer, Herbert, Walter Gropius,
and Ise Gropius, eds.
*Bauhaus,
1919-1928.*
New York: The Museum
of Modern Art,
1938.
Berger, John.
Ways of Seeing.
London: British Broadcasting
Corporation and Penguin
Books,
1987.
Bringhurst, Robert.
The Elements of Typographic Style.
Vancouver: Hartley & Marks,
1992.

Caplan, Ralph.
By Design.
New York: McGraw-Hill
Publishers,
1982.
Chanzit, Gwen F.
*Herbert Bayer and Modernist Design
in America.*
Ann Arbor: UMI Research
Press,
1987.
Dair, Carl.
Design with Type.
New York: Pellegrini & Cudahy,
1952.
de Harak, Rudolph, ed.
*Posters by Members of the Alliance
Graphique Internationale 1960-1985.*
New York: Rizzoli
International,
1986.
Demeude, Hugues.
The Animated Alphabet.
New York: Thames & Hudson,
1996.
Drier, Thomas.
The Power of Print—and Men.
Brooklyn: Mergenthaler
Linotype Company,
1936.
Drucker, Johanna.
*The Visible Word: Experimental
Typography and Modern Art,
1909-1923.*
Chicago and London: The
University of Chicago Press,
1996.
Edwards, David.
How To Be More Creative.
San Francisco: Occasional
Productions,
1980.
Fern, Alan, and Mildred Constantine.
Word and Image.
New York: Museum of Modern
Art,
1968.
Forty, Adrian.
Objects of Desire: Design and Society.
London: Thames & Hudson,
1992.
Gill, Eric.
An Essay on Typography.
Boston: David R. Godine,
1989.
Gombrich, E.H.
The Image and the Eye.
Ithaca: Cornell University
Press,
1982.
Gombrich, E.H.
The Sense of Order.
Ithaca: Cornell University
Press,
1979.
Gregory, Richard L.
*Eye and Brain:
The Psychology of Seeing.*
Princeton: Princeton
University Press,
1990.

Heller, Reinhold.
Toulouse-Lautrec,
The Soul of Montmartre.
Munich: Prestel,
1997.
Heller, Steven, and Karen Pomeroy.
Design Literacy:
Understanding Graphic Design.
New York: Allworth Press,
1997.
Hochuli, Jost, and Robin Kinross.
Designing Books.
London: Hyphen Press,
1996.
Jaffe, Hans L.C.
De Stijl: 1917-1931.
Cambridge: Belknap Press,
1986.
Johnson, Pamela, ed.
The Journal of Decorative and
Propaganda Arts: Swiss Theme Issue.
No.19. 1993.
Julier, Guy.
Encyclopaedia of 20th Century
Design and Designers.
London: Thames & Hudson,
1993.
Kepes, Gyorgy.
The Language of Vision.
Chicago: Theobald,
1959.
Kinross, Robin.
Modern Typography. .
London: Hyphen Press,
1994.
Kramer, Hilton.
The Age of the Avant-Garde.
New York: Farrar, Strauss
and Giroux,
1973.
Le Corbusier.
The Modulor 1 and The Modulor 2.
Cambridge: Harvard
University Press,
1980.
Le Corbusier.
Towards a New Architecture.
New York: Dover Press,
1986.
Lemaire, Gérard-Georges.
Calder.
New York: Harry N. Abrams
Publishers,
1997.
Lissitzky-Kuppers, Sophie.
El Lissitzky.
New York: Thames & Hudson,
1980.
Livingston, Alan and Isabella.
Dictionary of Graphic Designers
and Design.
London: Thames & Hudson,
1992.
Margadant, Bruno.
Das Schweizer Plakat / The Swiss
Poster / L'affiche Suisse,
1900-1983.
Basel: Birkauser Verlag,
1983.

Marsack, Robin, ed.
Essays on Design 1:
AGI's Designers of Influence.
London: Booth-Clibborn
Editions,
1997.
McLean, Ruari.
Typographers on Type.
London: Lund Humphries,
1995.
Meggs, Philip.
A History of Graphic Design.
New York: Van Nostrand
Reinhold,
1992.
Monguzzi, Bruno.
Piet Zwart:
The Typographical Work 1923-1933.
Milan: Rassegna,
1979.
Müller, Lars, ed.
Josef Müller-Brockmann, Designer.
Baden: Verlag Lars Müller,
1995.
Murphy, Diana, ed.
The Work of Charles and Ray Eames:
A Legacy of Invention.
New York: Harry N. Abrams,
1997.
Panofsky, Erwin.
Meaning in the Visual Arts.
Chicago: University of
Chicago Press,
1982.
Papanek, Victor.
Design for the Real World.
Chicago: Academy of
Chicago Publishers,
1985.
Rand, Paul.
A Designer's Art.
New Haven: Yale University
Press,
1985.
Rothstein, Julian, and Mel Gooding.
Alphabets & Other Signs.
Boston: Shambhala,
1995.
Rotzler, Willy, Fritz Schärer,
and Karl Wobmann.
Das Plakat in der Schweiz.
Zurich: Ex Libris,
1991.
Ruder, Emil.
Typographie.
Teufen: Verlag Arthur Niggli,
1967.
Schapiro, Meyer.
Theory and Philosophy of Art.
New York: Braziller,
1994.
Schmalenbach, Werner.
Kurt Schwitters.
New York: Harry N. Abrams
Publishers,
1967.
Sontag, Susan.
Against Interpretation and Other
Essays.
New York: Anchor Press,
1990.

Tschichold, Jan.
The New Typography.
Berkeley: University
of California Press,
1996.
Warncke, Carsten-Peter.
The Ideal as Art : De Stijl 1917-1931.
Köln: Taschen,
1998.
Zinsser, William.
On Writing Well.
New York: Harper-Collins
Publishers,
1994.

Bruno Monguzzi: A Designer's Perspective is the second volume in the series *Issues in Cultural Theory*, to be published annually by the Fine Arts Gallery, University of Maryland, Baltimore County. This book, an extensive evaluation of the work of the innovative Swiss designer, exemplifies the goal of the series to explore the broader social, political, and aesthetic issues around contemporary cultural practices. Closely examining Monguzzi's typographical inventions, as well as his theoretical tracts and designs for packaging household objects, pavilions, books, and even for Swiss currency, curator Franc Nunoo-Quarcoo demonstrates the greater influence that design can effect on the look, sensibility, and direction of everyday life.

This book also demonstrates the central role that design itself plays in the visual and intellectual sensibility of *Issues in Cultural Theory*. In his design for this catalogue, Monguzzi puts his intellectual perspective into practice, brilliantly suggesting the theoretical content of this exhibition through the visual sensibility of the book. The innovative designs of the volumes in this series have placed them in the forefront of American book design, earning the series' first title, *Minimal Politics: Performativity and Minimalism in Recent American Art*, this country's most prestigious honors for book design.

The Fine Arts Gallery is committed to supporting progressive and demanding projects such as *Bruno Monguzzi: A Designer's Perspective*. Forthcoming editions will explore the work and theory of conceptual artist and philosopher Adrian Piper and designer Paul Rand as well as the issue of the shifting role of the spectator in contemporary art.

Maurice Berger
Series Editor
Issues in Cultural Theory
Fine Arts Gallery
University of Maryland
Baltimore County

Issues In Cultural Theory

Series Editor
    Maurice Berger
Managing Editor
    Antonia LaMotte Gardner

Fine Arts Gallery

Executive Director
    David Yager
Director of Programs
    Symmes Gardner
Adjunct Curator
    Maurice Berger
Projects Coordinator
    Monika Graves

Design
    Bruno Monguzzi

Typesetting
    Sergio Taiana

Photography
    Alberto Flammer
    Franco Mattei

Printing
    Schmitz Press
    Sparks, Maryland